I
HOPE
YOU'RE
HAVING A
GREAT
DAY!

I KNOW I AM!

PAM CHRISTIAN

BALBOA.PRESS

A DIVISION OF HAY HOUSE

Balboa Press books may be ordered through booksellers or by contacting:

Balboa Press
A Division of Hay House
1663 Liberty Drive
Bloomington, IN 47403
www.balboapress.com
844-682-1282

Print information available on the last page.

ISBN: 979-8-7652-4342-8 (sc)
ISBN: 979-8-7652-4341-1 (e)

Library of Congress Control Number: 2023911907

Balboa Press rev. date: 03/14/2024

PREFACE

People have been telling me to write a book for as long as I can remember. My life has definitely been colorful, so I understand why they think it would be a good idea. But what would I say? Where would I start? With my childhood or with where I am now? Okay, there I go overthinking again. Maybe it's just not in the cards at this point. But wait! I am giving all this guidance to others to push through, to keep going. Why should I let myself off the hook? So, here it goes.

My life could be compared to a roller coaster – moments of sheer terror and moments of euphoria. As I have gotten older, I have learned to lean into the happiness and also to be open to the moments of terror so that I can go deeper, get to know myself better and evolve into a person who can both be fully immersed in life and help others immerse themselves in their own lives. This is what I want for you! We certainly can't control all of life's events, as much as many of us want to, and surrendering a little can yield a surprisingly rewarding outcome.

While this sounds easy, my journey has been anything but. Yet it has also been vibrant, rich, rewarding and relatable – I am sure you can relate already!

You can read this book in one of two ways: It is my story, and you can read it just for that. Or, at the end of each chapter, you can implement the tips I include, which I have also used to overcome various traumas and challenges. No matter how you read this, I hope there are lots of takeaways for you. I also hope that whatever difficulties lie in front of you, you know you have the power to overcome them. I am not saying that it will be easy or that there won't be setbacks. I am saying that I know you can do it. Whether you know me personally or not, I am rooting for you every step of the way.

This book was truly a labor of love. As I wrote it, it brought up many painful memories alongside happy ones. While I thought I had worked through the various layers of my life, I came to understand that the work never ends. As we shed one set of layers and level up, we gain a new lens through which we see those experiences differently. And, once again, we have to work through those emotions. It may sound exhausting – and it can be – but it is also beautiful, fulfilling and empowering. It is life.

When I decided to write this book, I felt that if my story could help just one person, then I would have accomplished what I set out to do. I was scared to put it all out there because, although I am in the best place I have ever been and I love who I am today as well as the girl I was, I still have shame and embarrassment about what I went through. Writing helped me to relive and process my experiences. It helped me to love and appreciate myself. It helped me to understand what I had been through and what I continue to go through. It helped me connect with my parents, whom I miss every day. It helped me recognize how much I have to be grateful for, and it helped me really connect with the warrior inside myself. May you find reading this to be equally empowering.

ACKNOWLEDGMENTS

Creating this book has been painful, exciting, difficult and liberating all at the same time. While I was writing it, I wasn't sure if or when I would publish it, but I kept on writing, knowing that I could decide later on. And while it's intimidating to put all of this out in the world, it's worth it if it can help someone else.

Some days were easier than others, whether it was from an emotional standpoint or just getting the thoughts and words down on paper. That being said, every day of this journey was made easier with the support and love of the following people whom I am eternally grateful to have in my life:

AJ, Jess and Michael: My true inspirations! I adore and love each of you more than words could ever convey. I am so grateful I get to be your mom.

Cara: My ride-or-die from day one. I love you so much!

Larry: I mean, could I really even have done this without your support? My dad would be so grateful for the way you have taken care of first my mom, my sister and me; and now my sister and me. I love you.

Liz: You are an unparalleled editor. Thank you for creating a beautiful, kind, supportive and caring space for me to explore this part of my life. I appreciate you!

Mom and Dad: Without you, none of this would have been possible. Thank you for pushing me to keep fighting and to never give up.

CHAPTER 1

I was born to loving parents who were eagerly awaiting the arrival of their second daughter, ME. But of course my story, like anyone else's, begins even before my birth. My parents met on a blind date through a mutual friend in the '70s. My dad always said he knew right away that my mom was the one. My mom, on the other hand, wasn't so sure. My dad was recently divorced with no children and was looking for a woman who would complement him and make him a better version of himself. Maybe it was my dad's ambition, or maybe it was their shared background (both of my parents came from low-income families in New York), but eventually my mom came around and, within nine months, they were married. Their vision for the future was aligned with only one major difference: My mom wanted children and my dad did not. But he was willing to have them if it meant that he and my mom would spend their lives together.

Married life was pleasant and pretty simple for them. They had no money to their name, and they lived in a tiny apartment in Rockaway, Queens, until they found out they were pregnant with me. At that point, they moved to a new, middle-class development in New Jersey.

In some ways, my early childhood was relatively straightforward. My older sister was without any major issues, my mom was a traditional homemaker and my dad was the breadwinner. He was a typical patriarch of the time: working hard and away much of the time doing so. When he was home, he was working, supporting our extracurricular activities, or drinking a JD and 7UP and enjoying a cigar. Even our dog was great! But I was a handful once the baby phase ended. By the age of 5 or 6, I was struggling socially and academically with self-esteem and impulsivity issues. I would make up stories and intentionally annoy people so they would leave me alone. I had become an expert at closing my heart and putting up my guard. (That's something I now work on daily – opening up and breaking down the walls that I spent years building. Funny how that happens.)

As the days, weeks, months and years went by, my parents did not know what to do with me. They loved me, and they wanted the best for me, but they simply did not have the tools or resources to handle me. As a parent with three kids of my own, I do feel for what they endured. They tried everything they possibly could to "fix" the situation and, even though they truly were progressive for the time, nothing could prevent me from the self-sabotaging and destructive behavior I inflicted on myself and everyone around me.

While nothing felt normal about me, my world or my life, no one would guess it from the outside because we seemed like a typical family. My dad, like many fathers back then, commanded attention and compliance by his mere presence. But he took his authority further than most. He was a dictator: When he spoke, we listened. Actually, everyone listened whether they wanted to or not. To say he was intimidating would be a gross understatement. He was larger than life in many ways, and how he interacted with people and the world in general was heavily dependent on his moods. He could be generous and fun; he could also be explosive, obsessive and overbearing. Part of this aspect of his personality can be chalked up to his addiction issues. He stopped drinking alcohol around the time I turned 8, but the same behaviors – the taunting, the lashing out, the anxiety – remained. He was what is commonly referred to as a "dry drunk": Even when he abstained from alcohol, he often acted like an angry alcoholic anyway. He would go on to relapse in 2005 after 20 years of sobriety, which was heartbreaking because he wanted to be stronger than that.

My dad commuted to the city each day for work, so he wasn't around a ton, but when he was, he was the head honcho. My mom, on the other hand, was a homemaker who dabbled in social work on the side, always wanting to learn, grow and improve herself. (Wonder where I got it from!)

By the time I was 5 years old, my parents were understandably at their wits' end with me. My lack of compliance was compounded by the fact that my older sister was what was considered by my parents, relatives and really anyone who knew her as "the golden child." I know that label has its own pressures and issues but, up to that point, it had been mostly great for her. I often felt that life was so unfair because, while she was on top of the world, I was at the bottom of a very deep hole, barely surviving let alone thriving. Have you ever had one of those dreams where you're trying to scream for help but nothing comes out? That's how I felt almost every day.

But there was an explanation for this that had nothing to do with who I was and everything to do with what was happening to me. You see, I had a very dark and scary secret: From the time I was about 3 to 10 years old, I was being sexually abused by a family member.

Sexual abuse can be defined in a number of ways. The key characteristics, according to the psychotherapist and author Wendy Maltz, center on domination, coercion and exploitation. For me, it involved a trusted adult family member who robbed me of my childhood, my sense of security and my innocence. Despite the fact that I am finally here, on the other side, it sure didn't feel like I would ever get here.

I was so young when the abuse started that it was really all I ever knew. Even as I instinctively felt that it was wrong, I was too scared to say anything. I was scared that my abuser would hurt me or my family. Obviously that's unrealistic, but I was just a little girl. What did I know? I was scared that my parents would be mad at me. I was scared to disrupt things, which I was doing anyway, just differently. I was scared that no one would believe me. I used to lie and make up stories to escape the reality of my own life, so it was always difficult for people to know when I was telling the truth. And, most of all, I was ashamed of myself for letting the abuse happen.

So it continued for many years. I would dream about someone walking in and catching us but that never happened. I remember this relative would come over to visit. We'll call him Dave. Dave would put on his public face and have "tickle time" in front of my family with me and my cousins. Everyone had so much fun and thought he was this amazing relative, but they had no idea about the darkness that lived inside of him and in which he immersed me. What's so crazy is that, in retrospect, the signs were there.

If only my parents could have known or, if they did know on some level, had been able to admit it to themselves and then act on it. Everything would've been different. I just wanted someone to help! I wanted to be saved! There were so many indicators – why were my parents missing them? I was afraid of my own shadow, and I was constantly complaining about something. It was too hot out, it was too cold out, there wasn't enough of this, there was too much of that. My stomach always hurt, and I didn't want to go to school most days. When I did go to school, I spent much of the time in the nurse's office. No surprise then that my teachers were regularly reaching out to my parents about my grades, lack of interest in school and overall behavioral issues. I went to the pediatrician all the time, yet no one – not my parents, not my doctor, not my teachers – wondered why, at such a young age (we are talking nursery and elementary school), I was getting yeast infections, why I was depressed, why I had insomnia, why I had no friends, why I was constantly ridiculed and teased and bullied. I now know that I brought it on myself by the way I was acting out. But back then, I was just a little girl trying to survive. I had no idea why these things were happening to me, and why I couldn't just be "normal."

Instead of looking at external factors as the potential cause, everyone looked at me. I brought the negative attention on myself, it seemed, and then had a victim mentality. But how could that be at such a young age? This was also a time when, in the late '70s and early '80s, children were meant to be seen and not heard. I simply didn't have the necessary coping skills. I'm not sure any child ever does. And so, instead, I constantly asked myself why couldn't I change, why couldn't I be better, why couldn't I be easier to deal with? I hated myself.

My parents did not, maybe could not, face the possibility of abuse, but they did seek help. They acknowledged that my dad's volatility, and my mom's passive response to it, might've played a role in my behavior. Otherwise, they assumed I was the one at fault. I was simply born the problem child, the bad one.

TIPS & TAKEAWAYS

Finding Your Inner Voice

There's an old story attributed to the Cherokee tribe in which a grandfather tells his grandson, "There is a battle between two wolves inside us all. One is Evil. It is anger, jealousy, greed, resentment, inferiority, lies and ego. The other is Good. It is joy, peace, love, hope, humility, kindness, empathy and truth."

The boy considered this and then asked, "Grandfather, which wolf wins?"

The old man replied, "The one you feed."

There was always that inner voice in my head. Actually, there was more than one, and although I was always able to hear the one that would serve me well, it would take me years before I would listen to it. I was not strong enough to listen to it. Instead, I fed the inner voice that spoke to my insecurities and anxieties. I listened to my inner critic, my saboteur who would tell me that what was happening was my fault, that I was gross and that I deserved it. Your true inner voice, though, is the one that guides you. Sometimes it is quiet and gentle and subtle; other times it is loud and urgent. To truly benefit from that voice, however, you have to access it, hear it and, most of all, trust it. These things take time. Today, it's the only voice I listen to.

How to find your healthy inner voice:

1. **Find quiet and acknowledge that you have an inner voice**: The quieter you are, the more you can hear. This skill takes time to develop because, when you first find quiet, your mind will likely still be noisy. You have to find quiet on a daily basis to remove the noise of fear, worry and limiting beliefs, and let your true inner voice speak out. Press pause on this moment so you can slow down, get to know yourself and tune in.

2. **Act on one thing your inner voice says**: Take a step and see how it works out.

3. **Be willing to accept the teacher who shows up**: Once the chatter and noise have dissipated, your teacher can and will show up. This teacher will be some form of your higher self. Be open and receptive.

CHAPTER 2

What was wrong with me? One of the endless assessments I underwent concluded that I had some learning issues. I'm not sure what the formal diagnosis was, but I was labeled with a learning disability (now referred to as a "learning disorder") that, we were informed, was likely at the root of my behavioral problems. It's kind of comical looking back on that now, because my parents believed that treating this disorder would fix everything! They were excited and ready to develop a structured plan that, they thought, would finally set me on the right course in life. What's interesting is that there is a direct correlation between childhood sexual abuse and academic problems. As many as 48 percent of sexually abused girls ages 7 to 12 will earn below-average grades, and abused children of both sexes routinely score lower on tests measuring cognitive ability and memory assessments. Victims of childhood sexual abuse are also more likely to require special-education services and less likely to finish high school and attend or finish college.

The situation is especially sobering for boys. At least one in six boys will have experienced sexual abuse before the age of 16, although that number is likely much higher owing to a cultural reticence around speaking out. Studies also indicate that the sexual abuse of boys directly correlates with both learning disorders and poor academic performance.

All the signs pointed toward sexual abuse in my case, but instead I was diagnosed with a learning disability and had to start a treatment plan for that. Great! Just keep on adding to my self-esteem, why don't you? I was still in elementary school, and the protocol for my diagnosis was to regularly pull me out of my mainstream class for specialized assistance. Isn't there a better system than pulling a kid out of her class to get extra help? How humiliating! Regardless of how old you are, if you are relatively mainstream and highly functioning, and you get pulled out of class for additional academic help, there is an immediate stigma attached to you. And let me tell you, kids notice and kids are cruel! When you are a kid, all you want to do is fit in. Having to be pulled out of class, or being singled out for help in class, makes you feel like you are anything but normal, and it puts a target on you. Breaking off from the group to go to these classes was a constant reminder that I was different from the rest of the kids, and that made me jealous and angry. These emotions and experiences would later contribute to my low self-esteem and self-destructive behavior.

I personally had to deal with this only in elementary school, but I have coached many adults who were traumatized by that system after enduring it throughout middle and high school. Their peers relentlessly made fun of them, other people devalued them because they did not fit the mold of the traditional learner and they themselves felt like they were not good enough or smart enough. I now know that there is no one-size-fits-all for learning, and I am kind of glad that I didn't conform to the traditional education system. It is an antiquated and flawed system based on an antiquated and flawed model. However, as children, we are not aware or strong enough to understand that fitting in with the norm in no way reflects how smart we are. I became identified by my learning disorder and by my difficult behavior, but never by who I truly was.

My parents, meanwhile, were happy to finally have a diagnosis. Yes, in a show of support, they learned everything they could about it. But they also used it to excuse or explain me to others. And they frequently relied on it when confronting me about something. It was a foolproof argument for whatever case they were trying to make. Hearing how defective I was, and how many weaknesses I had, began to wear on my nerves, my self-esteem and my overall well-being.

By the age of 7, I started to turn to food for comfort. Another classic sign that things were out of alignment. I wanted so badly for it to be different. I would eat when I was happy, which wasn't often, and when I was sad, when I was embarrassed and when I was made fun of. I even remember being at the dinner table when my parents would argue or say something that hit a nerve, and I would just stuff the food in. I couldn't even taste it. I was just trying to numb the emotions that were being triggered.

I felt like I was constantly letting down everyone around me, and it was demoralizing. It's hard to climb out when you feel like you're in a war zone, attacked from every angle (the sexual abuse, the learning differences, the verbal abuse from my father, my father's volatility and alcoholism, my mother's enablement of my father's destructive behavior). To cope, I sought out a variety of mechanisms: thumb-sucking, biting my nails until my fingers bled, negative self-talk and food. (My relationship with food would change over time. First, I overindulged. Later on, I would restrict my intake. Neither way was healthy, and it would take me some years to develop the balanced relationship with food and my body that I enjoy today.) And of course there were a variety of other self-destructive behaviors that got me in trouble all the time.

Because much of my childhood was so sad, the moments of pure joy really stand out. One of these joyful experiences concerned a stray German shepherd that regularly passed by our home and seemed to take an interest in me. The dog would not leave, and after we unsuccessfully tried to find its owner, we weren't exactly sure what to do. The dog, whom I named Rusty because of his coat, would visit us each day and quickly became my best friend and confidant. He brought me happiness and love in a very dark time.

I could relate to Rusty, just roaming around lost and only wanting to give love but being so misunderstood. He was loyal and loving, and I needed that light.

Though he wasn't allowed in the house, he stayed in our yard, and I fed him and took care of him. I was developing a strong bond with him, so when my dad said we couldn't keep him (we already had a dog), I was devastated. I begged my mom to find a way to stand up to my dad, advocate for me and make Rusty a part of our family. I looked forward to seeing Rusty in the morning before school and right when I got home from school, and I embraced the responsibilities of feeding and walking him because I loved him so much. My mom, however, was unable to change my dad's mind. The day we dropped him at the shelter was heartbreaking for me, and I remember my heart closing a little. The 20-minute car ride home felt like hours. I just stared out the window wondering how, on top of everything else, my best friend could be taken away from me. What, I wondered, had I done wrong to deserve this pain? And, throughout it all, the sexual abuse continued. I remember specific incidences in my bedroom, in the bathtub, in the parking lot of Dave's apartment building and in his apartment on his pull-out couch. By that point, it had happened so many times that, when I heard his footsteps, I would start to dissociate. It was almost like an out-of-body experience. I would enter a trance-like state until he left the room. Only then would I return to myself, crying, scared, sick to my stomach and alone.

I wish I could articulate my exact feelings but they were, ultimately, indescribable. It was a completely physical experience, and words fail to express it accurately. Of course, there were many emotions that surrounded the abuse. There was fear (of him) and disgust (toward both him and myself), but the actual moments of violation were a trauma that was purely visceral. Only other victims could truly understand what I am talking about.

One experience stands out in particular. I was probably 8 or 9, and I had to spend the night with him in his apartment for some unremembered reason. I vividly recall the parking lot of his apartment complex: He lived in a high-rise in Fort Lee, New Jersey, and the parking lot was located under the building. It was dark in that parking lot, and there were lots of cars but no other people besides the two of us. I was out of the car and carrying my overnight bag over my shoulder. It was heavy, so I was kind of leaning toward one side out of balance. A part of me was looking forward to the adventure. Dave came over to me, wearing tan pants, a light blue cashmere sweater and a white collared shirt underneath. He clapped his hands and rubbed them together with this excited look on his face as he said, "Hey, Monkey." "Monkey" was his nickname for me. It makes me cringe just thinking about it now. He touched me in a way that made my skin crawl, telling me that we were going to have a fun weekend. The way he said that turned my anticipation into fear. I knew what I was in for that night.

At that point, I had surrendered to the fact that I would be spending the weekend with this person and, as a survival mechanism, I tuned out what I knew would inevitably happen later on. Everything was "normal" until I got into bed that evening. The apartment was very small and there was a pull-out couch where I would sleep. We had finished dinner, and he was cleaning up in the kitchen, which was combined with the den where I was watching TV and where I would sleep that night. I could hear him whistling and humming to himself. That whistle will always be etched in my mind. When I hear a whistle today that even mildly resembles his whistle, I get triggered. My stomach was starting to churn. His footsteps drew closer, and then there he was, lying in bed next to me, stroking me. Talking to me. Acting like he cared while touching me all over. It always hurt – he was so rough and then, just like that, he was done. He lay there spooning me, pressed against my back while I desperately wished him away. He got up and asked me if I wanted ice cream but, as was the routine at that point, I just pretended to be asleep.

Where were my parents? Why was I alone with no one to protect me, no one to protect the little girl who just wanted some normalcy in her life? I remember realizing at that moment that I was in this by myself and that, going forward, no one would be there for me. I would have to take care of myself for the rest of my life; I couldn't rely on anyone else.

The revulsion I felt toward my abuser and, more importantly, toward myself hurt then and hurts today as I write this. At a young age, I began to build emotional walls around myself so that I could endure the abuse while not letting it permeate my heart, not letting it break me. I remember the dread and terror leading up to and after the experiences, and how that terror leaked into my everyday life. I would cry at night because I was so terrified – terrified that the monster would find me again. And, paradoxically, terrified that he would not. I know it sounds crazy but it is a classic symptom of sexual abuse and one that is well articulated by Elizabeth Hartney, PhD, in her article, "The Cycle of Sexual Abuse and Abusive Adult Relationships." "If the connection between abuse and 'love' is made early in life," she writes, "the feelings of shame and anger, which naturally happen as a consequence of the abuse, can become mixed up with sexual feelings, leading to confusion in the person who experienced the abuse. These feelings may become interpreted as feelings of love and passion."

I was ashamed of the abuse for so long. But as much as I didn't want it to continue, I also started to wonder what was wrong with me if he didn't come back. Questions like "Why doesn't he love me anymore? Why doesn't he want me?" would make me feel even worse about myself. It is a cycle that messes with your head.

Because my abuser was simultaneously someone who was a monster and someone whom I had adored, admired and loved, I suffered a great deal of inner conflict. He was the only person at the time who treated me like I meant something, who made me feel special and who didn't define me by my "issues" (many of which, ironically, were created by him). When you are so young, the mixed messages can be confusing.

To be honest, I still find it very confusing. I have been through lots of deep therapy to move on and become closer to the person I was meant to be, to my authentic self, but the abuse is something I will always carry with me as it has affected every facet of my life. And while I wish it hadn't happened to me, I also always knew there was a reason behind it and that, at some point, I would use it to help people.

TIPS & TAKEAWAYS

Boosting Your Self-Esteem

Self-esteem is defined as confidence in one's own worth or abilities. The experiences I had during my formative years set the stage for my self-esteem, or how I felt about myself. Being pulled out of classes, not getting along with my peers, having a volatile and alcoholic parent and being viewed by my parents as the problem child all wore away at my self-esteem. Add in the sexual abuse, and the odds were clearly stacked against any healthy sense of self-worth.

My low self-esteem manifested itself in ways that were both self-destructive and destructive to other people. Although I forgave myself a long time ago, I still feel sick when I think of how I treated myself and others. The climb out of that mental state was slow and messy, but eventually I was able to undo the damage and find a deep love, respect and admiration for myself and my strength. That is where I am today. No one deserves to feel anything but love, pride, happiness and joy about themselves.

To improve your self-esteem:

1. **Believe in the possibility of change**: In order to change, grow and feel better about yourself, you have to believe that change is possible!

2. **Say affirmations**: Start with "I am" and follow it up with something positive about yourself. A few examples are "I am beautiful," "I am smart," "I am healthy" and "I am love!"

3. **Challenge your limiting beliefs**: Don't take them at face value just because they are what come up for you. Question them to see if they hold water or just hold you back. Then, find opportunities to congratulate, compliment and reward yourself. You can start with small things like championing yourself when you make it to the gym or do something you've been avoiding, and grow from there.

4. **Stand at the edge of your comfort zone**: When you push yourself to the brink of what you think is possible (or beyond), you get to see what you are really made of. More often than not, you are capable of far more than you think you are.

5. **Heal your past**: The fastest and surest way to overcome your insecurities is by healing! Healing takes hard work, commitment and time, but going inward and working on yourself is where the magic happens. It's what lets you eventually drop the baggage and just be.

6. **Get clear on your values**: Knowing your values allows you to identify what is important. And don't expect your values to match up with mine. You might value leisure time, while I might value learning. The point is not what your values are but rather how you can live in a way that resonates with them. When you do this, you are living authentically, and you feel good about yourself.

7. **Don't worry about what others think**: Focusing on what others think distracts you from what is truly best for you, because it trains your attention on what other people value as opposed to what you know is right for you. Instead of

constantly chasing someone else's ideal of what is good or valuable, home in on what you value and go for it.

8. **Help someone out**: As Mahatma Gandhi so eloquently said, "The best way to find yourself is to lose yourself in the service of others." Research shows that giving, not just money but also time and effort, cultivates self-worth and makes us happy. It also reinforces our own values. Giving is living!

9. **Read inspirational material**: The information we ingest directly impacts how we feel about ourselves. Make sure what you are putting in your mind is positive and growth-oriented and moves you forward!

10. **Face your fears**: When you hide from your fears, they just get bigger and bigger. Face them, and more often than not you will realize they are probably not as scary in real life as they are in your head.

11. **Welcome failure**: It is impossible to achieve success without failure. Embrace failure over and over again. Not only will it bring you closer to success, it will also make you stronger, show you what you are made of and, over time, build your confidence in yourself and your potential.

CHAPTER 3

What they say is really true: "The only way out is through." Recovery wasn't easy, and it was definitely a process, but I am so glad I chose that path. If I hadn't, I don't know if I would have made it. I certainly wouldn't be the high-functioning, healthy adult that I am today.

I experienced post-traumatic stress disorder (PTSD) throughout my young adulthood until I finally shed my fears. The PTSD manifested itself in many ways, and while I would like to assign blame solely to my abuser, there were other factors as well, including my hostile-but-loving home environment. Yep, the two *can* coexist! I have worked so hard to rid myself of the anxiety, the constant looking over my shoulder and the guilt, loss and sadness. People often remark on my strength, whether they're referring to the incest or other things that I have endured. I know I am strong, but ultimately I was just following my intuitive guide. There is no way I could have gotten through everything without that inner voice leading me. I can't emphasize enough how important it is to find your inner voice and then trust it.

I remember one night when I was triggered more than usual. One of the pipes had burst in my family's home, and there was a flood, so we had to sleep out. I spent the night at a family friend's house while my sister went to a close friend's home, and my parents went to a hotel. The family I stayed with was great. They had two girls around my age, and we had a lot of fun until it was time for bed. I slept alone in the guest room. The dad came to check on me, and when he sat on the bed to talk, it triggered me. I spent the rest of the night crying and throwing up.

At the time, I couldn't figure out what was happening. But over the years, I have come to realize that I was petrified that the moment the dad sat down on the bed, there would be a repeat of the experiences I had endured with Dave. As a result, my body just shut down completely.

During this time in my life, the insomnia was relentless, the eating and stuffing my feelings down were numbing, the chronic "illnesses" were consuming, the lack of self-esteem was debilitating, the negative self-talk was hurtful and the fear, the constant fear, was overwhelming. I was always on edge, which made me hyper-aware of my surroundings. When I think about that little girl with her rounded shoulders, her head down, her disheveled and chubby appearance and her nails so short they were always bleeding, my heart absolutely breaks. I was so full of pain and sadness. No child should ever have to endure that kind of suffering or have their childhood stolen.

Sadly, I am not alone. So many children experience situations similar to or worse than mine, and the effects are profound. As psychotherapist and author Wendy Maltz outlines in her work, childhood sexual abuse can hinder normal social growth and cause numerous psychosocial problems. It correlates with higher levels of depression, guilt and shame, as well as self-blame, eating disorders, poor body image, somatic concerns, anxiety, dissociative patterns, repression, denial, sexual problems and relationship issues, just to name a few. Survivors often have feelings of worthlessness and avoid others because they believe they have nothing to offer. And those feelings of guilt, shame and self-blame can also cause survivors to take personal responsibility for the abuse.

I am fortunate that my parents were focused on helping me and offered me constant support, even though they couldn't pinpoint the source of my problems. But this trauma occurred at a pivotal time in my development and interrupted my path, preventing me from developing into my authentic self. As I grew up, I desperately wanted to get back to that person, the person I knew I could be, the person I knew I was meant to be, but how could I abandon that little girl who had suffered so much? The little girl who had been violated and exploited in the worst possible way at such a vulnerable age? Sexuality and intimacy are difficult on our best days. Robbing someone of a healthy relationship based on those foundations is utterly devastating. Even today I have intimacy issues.

Fortunately, I learned how to love and take care of that damaged little girl. Eventually, I was able to release her even though she will always be a part of the fabric of who I am. And, in some ways, she has been a blessing. She has taught me empathy, compassion, love, strength, resilience, perseverance, self-love, humility and the value of being nonjudgmental. She has taught me how to control my mind and find a way to be mentally strong amid the chaos that happens both internally and externally.

Dealing with the trauma of sexual abuse on top of the more garden-variety problems during my childhood (passive mom and a domineering, volatile, unpredictable, alcoholic and verbally abusive father) meant it was very confusing with so much stimulation and instability around me during that pivotal stage in my life. What I can say is that, despite the behavior and limitations of my parents, there is absolutely no question they loved me and wanted the best for me. They were doing the best they could in a time when parenting looked very different than it does today. Back then, the word *parenting* wasn't yet a verb. Children's lives revolved around those of the adults, as opposed to today's generation, for whom the opposite seems to be true. My parents, having been raised by parents who had survived the Depression, were dealing with their own demons. They grew up in a time when getting a beating with a belt was commonplace and when emotions were never talked about, let alone explored. Considering these circumstances and many other factors, it was easier for me to forgive my parents for the ways they failed me. They were not perfect, but their unwavering love and support gave me the foundation I needed to find my true self.

TIPS & TAKEAWAYS

Cultivating Self-Awareness

If I had to choose the most important tool in terms of growing past my trauma and developing into my authentic self, I would say it was self-awareness. The development of self-awareness, of consciousness, did not happen overnight. Not even close! It is something that has been and continues to be an ongoing process as it is for everyone. The most important factor for developing self-awareness is to get started. It will evolve as you evolve!

Self-awareness is about knowing yourself on a conscious level. Knowing your character, feelings, motives and desires. When I got to the point where I wanted to make adjustments to who I was, I had to take a hard look at myself and be honest. I did not like what I saw, which was very painful to admit. I knew at my core that I had certain values, but I was not living them. I was running from myself, hiding and living for everyone else, which was the worst thing I could do. Living in that space is not genuine and, at the time, it made me miserable as I constantly wrestled with inner turmoil.

Developing self-awareness is about falling in love with who you are and who you are becoming over and over again. It's about recognizing your strengths and, equally if not more importantly, recognizing your weaknesses, your triggers and your self-limiting beliefs. Only when you are self-aware are you able to refine the traits you like and understand why you react and respond to things the way you do.

Personally, understanding my reactions was absolutely key to making the necessary changes for me to live the life I wanted to live and become the person I wanted to be. If you are not in touch with this side of yourself, it is impossible to make changes. Being self-aware allows for personal growth and development. Without it, there is no room to enjoy your life on a higher level. Self-awareness facilitates deeper self-understanding, more self-compassion and self-love, and increased love for others. As a child and young adult, I had certain patterns I kept repeating, despite my desire to change. Until I became more self-aware and introspective, though, I was destined to keep pushing people away or letting my temper get the better of me. These behaviors stemmed from my defensiveness. They were based on self-preservation rather than self-awareness. Once I was able to identify the behaviors as patterns, however, I opened the door to self-awareness.

When I got that first glimpse of self-awareness, it revealed just how much of myself and my life was up to me. Self-awareness is a powerful tool that allows us to master our lives. Where you focus your thoughts, attention, emotions and personality dictates the direction in which they will grow, and this hugely influences how you live your daily life. The more self-aware you are, the more you can identify these thoughts as they occur, which means you have greater control over them. That control was a big incentive for me. The first step toward greater self-awareness is to acknowledge there is something you want to work on. The facade we like to present to the world and our own selves often prevents us from moving forward. That's why you have to take that hard look at yourself. I know I didn't like myself or my behaviors when I was younger, and part of that was on me. It was tied up in the circumstances that surrounded me and allowed me to live with a victim mentality, pretending that I had no control over how I handled things. Of course, I could not control my life's circumstances, but I could certainly gain control of my reaction to those circumstances. I could stop playing the victim. ("Poor me," etc.) I could stop living as a victim of mental and physical abuse. I could choose a new way.

Did I grow up in an abusive, explosive and volatile environment that was even more confusing because it was also loving and supportive? Absolutely. Did I grow up with regular sexual abuse where I was objectified and made to feel like I was bad because I was the one chosen by my abuser? Did I confide in the people who I thought would know what was best but who did nothing? Did these things impact me and possibly change the trajectory of my life? Absolutely. These are facts I cannot deny! But did I have to allow these circumstances to define who I was, thereby permitting the self-destructive behavior as well as the hurtful behavior to others? Absolutely not! Do you know why? The reason I did not have to let that control me is because of a beautiful word everyone has the power to tap into: CHOICE.

Once I realized I had a choice as to how I was going to react to the circumstances around me, I felt empowered and alive but also paralyzed, scared and overwhelmed. I realized I had a choice and control, but I did not know how to make the necessary changes so that past events no longer defined who I was or who I would become.

The tips below can help put you on a path to making those changes.

1. **Look at yourself objectively**: In order to do this, you have to first get clear on how you currently come across to others. Look from the outside in and ask yourself, "What would I think of myself if I met myself for the first time?" How, in other words, would you like your personality if you saw it in someone else? Try to be fair in your assessment. Are you generous and patient, or do you tend to get to that state only after a temper tantrum? Then ask yourself, "What are the positives and negatives associated which each of my characteristics?"

2. **Write down your goals, plans and priorities**: This will help you clarify your purpose, your big why, and it will help you create a road map to getting there.

3. **Reflect daily**: Reflecting allows us to change what we don't like and add more of what we do like. It allows us to get to know ourselves on an even deeper level.

4. **Practice meditation and mindfulness**: This will allow you to quiet the noise in your head that arises from the limiting beliefs, the saboteurs and the inner critics that can dominate our mind space. If you practice meditation consistently, you will eventually tap into who you are and what you want from life.

5. **Ask for feedback about yourself from people you trust**: Find people who know you well, and encourage them to be honest with you in sharing the good, the bad and the ugly. This can be painful to do, but the gain is potentially huge. Not only can other people offer valuable insight on ways you can improve yourself (and your life!), but they might even surprise you with observations about good qualities you didn't know you had. Reward their trust by listening and accepting what they have to say. If you react with anger, defensiveness or denial, no one wins.

CHAPTER 4

Manhattan! YES! Finally a chance to start fresh!

I was in fourth grade when we got the news that we would be moving from our small town in New Jersey to the big city. My dad was finally getting noticed in his career, and his long hours working and commuting had been taking a toll on the entire family. It was time for a change.

My parents approached telling my sister and me with their customary indifference to our feelings. They let us know in June, once school had ended and just days before we left for summer sleepaway camp, that we would be moving over the summer. They didn't seem to realize that it might be a good idea to engage us kids in the process rather than leave us without a voice in any of the decisions. For my sister, it was devastating. She was entering middle school and was surrounded by great friends. She was a top athlete and was academically gifted, so she pretty much "had it all" and had no interest in giving that up. I, on the other hand, was excited. I recognized the opportunity to reinvent myself and start over, something that's hard to do when you live in a small town. It was also my chance to hopefully escape the monster disguised as a relative.

We left our comfortable, modest home in New Jersey to live in a hotel in New York's Upper West Side while our apartment was renovated. Hotel living was strange and difficult but also exciting and new. All of New York, for that matter, was exciting and new! The homogenous and sometimes suffocating town where I spent my first 10 years had given way to the city's kaleidoscope of people, places, noises and smells. There were endless possibilities, a new level of independence and finally a light at the end of this very dark tunnel. We were on a bit of a high (with maybe the exception of my sister). Life had certainly changed quickly! This was my first lesson in understanding that life is fluid and that things can change moment to moment, for better or worse. I learned that we have a CHOICE, and choice is power. We can decide how we want things to go by adjusting our mindset and creating the reality we want. It may be easier said than done, but it is possible. How empowering is that?!

The apartment my parents had found was also in New York's Upper West Side. It was a complete fixer-upper, but it had the bones necessary to make it exactly what they wanted. Wow – it was so different from suburban life with the garage, stairs, basement, backyard, etc. The apartment was in a prewar building with two wings. Our wing had one apartment per floor, so instead of walking out of the elevator into a hallway with other apartments, we walked right into our apartment, which was pretty cool if you ask me.

This was all happening in the '80s, when a lot of high-profile people were choosing Manhattan as either a full-time or a bicoastal residence. The Upper East Side co-ops often rejected celebrities – especially the musicians – because they were concerned about late-night parties and lots of difficult personalities. This drove celebrities to the Upper West Side, where creative talent was better received. Unbeknownst to my parents, the building where they purchased their apartment wound up being a haven for A-list celebrities such as Tom Cruise and Nicole Kidman, Harrison Ford, Sting and Trudie, Lorne Michaels, Clive Davis, Pia Lindstrom, Paul Simon, Carrie Fisher, Celeste Holm, and Billy Joel and Christie Brinkley, to name a few.

Although I knew it was cool and my friends oohed and aahed over it, I don't think I realized the magnitude of this while I was growing up. Each and every one of these artists was not only warm and welcoming but also respectful, fun, quiet and an overall great neighbor. I know that people often look for the negative about celebrities, relishing stories that highlight their self-centered and disruptive behaviors, but I have to say that every one of the individuals mentioned above was nothing but gracious toward me and my non-celebrity family.

As a teenager, I would come home from parties almost always breaking curfew, and I would often bump into the amazing cast from *Saturday Night Live* along with the special guest. They would have just finished the show for the night and were going to hang with Lorne in his apartment. People like Chris Farley, Eddie Murphy, Bill Murray, Phil Hartman, Mike Myers, Randy Quaid, Dana Carvey, Gilda Radner, Jon Lovitz, Martin Short, Billy Crystal, Jane Curtin and Kevin Nealon – the classic '80s crew – would be walking into the lobby of the building along with me. They were awesome and funny!

Moments like these illustrate the seismic lifestyle shift our family experienced in moving to Manhattan. We went from your average, middle-class family who enjoyed spending a Saturday at the local flea market and eating at the Ground Round to socializing with extremely high-profile people and attending elite private schools. Most of my peers at school had grown up in that environment, but I was so out of my element. My parents, meanwhile, were loving every minute of it. It was almost as if it was all the validation they needed. You could tell they felt free and were living their best lives… for the time being.

TIPS & TAKEAWAYS

Optimizing Your Choices

For a long time, I did not recognize the many choices in my life, both on a macro level and on a micro, day-to-day level. I allowed myself to be taken with the wind wherever life would have me go. Many of us do this. We become passengers, or passive observers, of our own lives. That's fine when the ride is a good one. But when the ride is all uphill, it can break you.

It wasn't until I recognized the power and presence of choice in my life that anything changed. Sure, outside forces and experiences are always going to show up, and they can be powerful. However, they have no control over how I choose to respond. Once I realized that I had the power to change certain things in my life, I was able to change my entire life. And that is exactly what I did. I decided to shift my lens, choosing to look for the good, to find the good and to see the good as often as I could.

The choice to see the best and be our best is always the optimal one. That doesn't mean it's the easiest choice to make, but it allows us to forge ahead even in uncharted territory and acknowledge that we have influence, we are leaders, we have power and we have the ability to make the best of a change in circumstances.

The power of choice is enormous. Every day we are faced with decisions, from what to make for breakfast to how we engage with ourselves. For example, if you wake up each morning determined to engage meaningfully with yourself, if you congratulate yourself on your successes (you got to the gym, you made your deadline, you were a thoughtful and patient partner or parent), then you perpetuate that resonant lifestyle with every choice. If, on the other hand, you give in to your inner critic, if you succumb to your negative self-talk, if you engage in self-destructive behavior or if you ignore these choices altogether and simply choose the path of least resistance, which is usually the least beneficial long term, what do you think the result will be? You got it! You won't feel fulfilled or in alignment, and you will keep searching even when the answer is right in front of your face. So, you see, choice is everything, and the best part about it is that you are in complete control!

Here's how to choose the best for yourself:

1. **Focus on the big picture**: When it comes to making the impact you want, staying clear on your objective and maintaining your momentum is key. Everything else, like the details surrounding your goal, will fall into place, so don't get sidetracked by the small stuff. Focusing on the big picture allows you to keep your final destination front of mind. You stay in sync with your ultimate goal and avoid the distractions and doubt that come with obsessing over the details.

2. **Live your values**: Our values are the compasses that point us in the right direction when it comes to living our best lives. They ground and center us, and they give our lives purpose and meaning. This is why it is so important to have a clear understanding of what your values are. Once you are clear on your values, you can let them guide the way you live. It takes hard work and effort to live this way, but it also enriches your life in powerful ways, creating a sense of alignment that eventually leads to greater personal freedom.

3. **Meditate on it**: Go into your meditation as you normally would. If you don't have a meditation practice yet, start one! Center yourself through breath work, mala beads, repeating a mantra, etc., so you clear the noise and can watch the answer appear. This won't happen immediately, but the more you slow down and quiet your mind, the more the answers will come to you. Once fully relaxed, use the subject area as your focus. For example, if your focus area is happiness, think of something that makes you feel happy.

When your attention drifts, which it inevitably will, go back to the feelings of happiness.

4. **Ask yourself what you really want**: Once you know what you truly want in life, it is very hard to go back to anything else. This question is a powerful one because it elevates you and forces you to look past your day-to-day responsibilities. But answering this question also speaks to the part of ourselves that we don't usually tune in to. It requires trusting yourself and your subconscious. The answers will come in bits and pieces over time, so daily, ask yourself what you want, and don't give up when it feels like nothing is happening. You just need to keep at it.

CHAPTER 5

L ife in the city was exhilarating! I was on a constant high with newfound freedom. I could walk to and from school on my own, which was great, and stop at my favorite bodega for freshly squeezed orange juice and a snack. There were new people in and out of my life, and I was learning a lot. I felt like this was the break I needed, the break I deserved.

My parents had embraced their new independence, which included not having to drive us around anymore. We had the bus, subway and taxis to do that, and our after-school activities were typically on or around campus. Forget that the people on the bus and subway were pretty shady. In fact, I had two experiences that only reinforced the sense that I was attracting a certain kind of energy. Both happened on the bus but at separate times. Once when I was around 10 years old, the bus was so crowded that people were pushed up against each other like sardines. A man took his hand and started feeling my butt, literally running his hand up and down the center of it as if he were swiping a credit card. I froze. I didn't know what to do. I wanted to move and scream, but I was paralyzed! The second time was to the same effect but on my breast. I must've been 12 or 13, and by that point I was so disgusted, I vowed never to take the bus again.

While these incidents were difficult, they also made me street savvy. I learned how to walk, talk and act so that no one would ever bother me in that way again. And no one has! I mean, talk about the Me Too Movement. Situations like these happened all the time and are part of the reason why Me Too has gained such traction. Sexual predation is real and dangerous. But it is equally important not to assume all men are predators. I know firsthand what kind of damage sexual assault causes. I refuse to assign blame for such a serious crime to anyone unless he or she is undoubtedly guilty of it.

Though the move brought lots of amazing changes, some things stayed the same and some things got worse. I was making lots of friends, but I was still so self-loathing that I always managed to damage those relationships. In my darkest hours, I would have to face the flashbacks, the fear and the confusion. I rarely slept at night. Often my mom would lie with me, trying to understand what was going on and why I was dealing with such turmoil. But she always missed the mark. Eventually, my parents got me a new radio for my bedside table, and I would listen to radio talk shows all night. No move was going to make the trauma better, but it sure was a great distraction!

I took with me the self-fulfilling prophecy that something was wrong with me, that my different learning style meant I wasn't smart or capable, that I was less-than. I am sure I still sometimes say things to myself that I shouldn't, but generally I am so much more mindful of my words today, not only to myself but to my kids and to those around me. While I was growing up, though, everyone was always talking about my issues: my attention-seeking behavior, my learning issues, my self-esteem issues, my weight issues and my issues with the difference between fact and fiction. I could go on and on. And while it's fine that they talked about these things, it's not fine that they did so right in front of me, constantly! How could that possibly help? It just contributed to my diminished sense of self-worth. Labels are powerful things, and when we consistently use negative ones with ourselves, with our children or with others, it only reinforces those qualities or behaviors. You can't focus on someone's weaknesses and still expect her to grow into her best self. I'm not saying that we should ignore deficits or problems, but why not crowd out the negatives by focusing on the positives?

I am not sure why I convinced myself that moving to Manhattan would mean that we would no longer see Dave, but I did. So you can imagine my surprise when I saw him at a family event we were hosting at our new apartment. In my mind, I had left him behind with everything else when we moved. I had been getting good at that – learning to compartmentalize, pretending like things didn't exist. So when he showed up, I became a ball of nerves. How could he sit there and talk about how much he loved Bruce Springsteen as though nothing had ever happened? It was manipulative, and I felt like I was dying inside all over again. It was at that moment that I decided the abuse was never going to happen again.

During that visit, Dave cornered me in my bedroom closet and tried to touch me over my pants. But instead of being the scared little girl who let him do anything he wanted, I stood up for myself and for that little girl. I remember confronting him, telling him that he was never going to touch me again. But in reality, my memory fails me. I can't remember if I set the boundary nonverbally or if I actually told him. I like to think that I stood up to him, but I just can't be sure. What I do know, however, is that that day was the last day he ever touched me.

Not long afterward, Dave and my dad had a falling out over other issues, and he was around less and less, which was fine by me. I would hear my mom and dad fight about him occasionally, but he was no longer a pervasive presence in my life. This gave me the room I needed to start the long journey toward figuring out who my authentic self was.

TIPS & TAKEAWAYS

Redefining Labels

From as early as I can remember, I have been pigeonholed by a variety of different labels. I took those labels on, allowed them to define who I was and then, for a very long time, I lived up, or down, to them in what became a self-fulling prophecy. Of course, when labels are imposed upon us at such a young age by family and friends, it is hard to fight against them. But there comes a time when we can wake up and decide the labels no longer fit or, even better, that they never did. We always have a choice, and we can decide to challenge, redefine or reject the labels we are assigned.

Imagine walking around all day being told you have a learning disability and that you are slow, that you are annoying and that no one likes you, that you are the problem child and why can't you be more like so-and-so. What if instead we set up positive labels for each other? How much healthier would we be? If we are willing to limit ourselves with negative labels, just imagine what would be possible if we lived up to positive ones!

To rewire your brain for a more positive frame of mind:

1. **Become aware**: The more we bring awareness into our state of being, the more we can build up our strengths and change our weaknesses. Awareness also brings with it a freedom from set beliefs and formulas. Suddenly, you can see yourself in a different light. You can take a new perspective on yourself that will ultimately lead you to a better life.

2. **Believe that your brain can change**: Many people believe that our brains are hardwired to function a certain way and that we don't have power beyond that. In reality, research suggests our brains are much more malleable than we once thought. The catch? If we don't believe we can change our

brains, then we definitely won't be able to. Think about it like a radio station. When you are listening to the radio and you don't like the song, you change the station. The same goes for our minds. If you don't like what you're hearing, change the "station" in your head. It's time to tune in to an internal frequency that promotes a healthy mindset.

3. **Challenge your thoughts**: Stop taking your thoughts at face value! This is one of our biggest misunderstandings: Just because we have a thought doesn't make it true. In fact, that couldn't be further from the truth. Go within, explore your thoughts, your feelings, your emotions and your beliefs to see if they still fit. Decide if they ever really fit. Challenge them, question them and course-correct accordingly!

4. **Practice gratitude**: Studies show that there is a direct correlation between happiness and gratitude. Gratitude allows us to focus on what we have rather than what we don't, and that gives you a greater shot at contentment. We all have something to be grateful for, even if it is as simple as life itself. Even better, gratitude begets more gratitude, meaning that the more you focus on gratitude (for your life, for your health, for your relationships, etc.), the more you find to be grateful for. No wonder happiness stems from gratitude!

5. **Get more sleep**: Sleep is a critical component of everyone's overall health and well-being. At the same time, it is also one of the most overlooked and dismissed. But sleep is crucial because it is our reset button. It allows our bodies to repair and ready themselves for another day. A good night's sleep can maximize performance in all areas of our lives, including emotions, social interactions and how we feel about ourselves in general. Feeling well rested and more positive about yourself lays the foundation for rewiring your brain into a more positive state of being.

6. **Monitor your self-talk**: Self-talk is the framework we use to create our lives. If your thoughts are typically negative, then that's what you can expect to get. But change that inner dialogue to a more positive script, and guess what? Your life becomes more positive. We each manifest the lives we are living, whether they are the lives we want or don't want. A big part of manifesting comes from our thoughts. Change your thoughts, change your life! This isn't as easy as it sounds, of course. You have programmed your brain to think a certain way. But your brain is like a motherboard: With a few tweaks, you can rewire it. It just comes down to you deciding to make those tweaks and then putting that decision into action.

7. **Know your purpose**: When you know your purpose, your life takes on a greater sense of meaning. With your purpose firmly in mind, you know what you love to do, what feeds you, what you are good at and how you can contribute to the world. If you don't yet know your purpose, don't worry. Part of the beauty of knowing your purpose is the journey you take to discover it. And, as a bonus, doing the introspective work to get to know your purpose always includes a shift between who you thought you were and who you really are. This shift naturally allows you to rewire your brain.

8. **Take steps to achieve your goals**: Knowing your goals and taking action toward achieving them are two completely different things. As you begin to move toward your goals, you will experience both successes and mistakes, both of which allow you to better get to know yourself. As you jettison the mask you once presented to the world, you will find resonance within yourself. Your brain will naturally begin to undo the damage, the programming and the patterns that have built up over the years, rewiring itself into a more authentic, joyful and positive state of being.

CHAPTER 6

I was doing better than I had been in New Jersey. By the time I was 11 years old, things were going well despite the fact that I was still struggling with self-esteem, academics and overall behavior. I think part of the reason why things improved was because my parents were now preoccupied with their own lives and that, in turn, allowed for a little more freedom for me. The first time I skipped school I was in sixth grade, and it wasn't remotely exciting: I went to the local library. But the funny thing was it felt great even though it was just the library! The beauty of New York City was the anonymity it afforded. A small-town librarian might be suspicious of why I wasn't in school. In New York, no one batted an eye.

The thing about my acting out was that I always got caught, because I never thought it through. Of course, the school would call when I didn't show up, right? And, of course, my parents would then find out. The fact was I simply didn't care.

My father, on the other hand, cared about a lot. Due to increasing demands at work and the new lifestyle he and my mom were enjoying, my dad's moods began to grow darker and more unpredictable. The yelling and screaming and conflict that surrounded me as I grew up left me in constant fight-or-flight mode. My father was someone who was truly ruled by his emotions, and while he worked on that later in life and did get better at it, he was always a prisoner of his own moods. Some days he would come home and be on such a high that the night would go perfectly. It meant a great family dinner, homemade popcorn on the couch and TV time together. But most nights, if there were a cup left out or shoes not put away or something else not to his satisfaction, he would explode. The screaming and the yelling would be followed by hours of damage control with his repetitive and desperate apologies. I know he was truly sorry for his actions while he was apologizing, but it was a vicious cycle. The same thing would happen the next night and the next night so that his apologies grew hollow and nothing changed. For him, each outburst was like a flipped switch. He would react and then, once he let it out, the switch would flip back and he assumed everything would just go back to normal. He felt better after venting his frustration, but the person on the receiving end was left with a whirlwind of emotions.

One particularly bad example was when he broke down the door to my bedroom. I can't remember what that fight was about. It could have been anything from a bad grade, to not having the napkin on my lap at the dinner table, to forgetting to walk the dog, to not cleaning up after myself. Whatever the cause, I ran to my room, slammed the door and tried to barricade it closed with my body. I just wasn't strong enough, though. My dad eventually broke it down, hinges and all, and I was terrified and angry. I ended up lying in my bed, crying. He came in and apologized, and I accepted, but I knew some version of the same thing would happen again.

My father was extremely intimidating. He was a leader, but people followed him out of fear. He felt in control and powerful when others were afraid of him. I remember occasions when we would be in the car as a family, and if my sister or I would crack our knuckles or make a noise that irritated him, he would turn around with such anger and disgust on his face and raise his arm as if he were going to hit us. He never did hit us – he made that vow when we were very young – but the threat of it was just as traumatizing as a physical blow. For him, it was over as quickly as it started, but for us, the fear remained, building up and hardening us in ways that kids should not have to be hardened.

It was such a complicated situation because his love for us was real and abundant but so was the abuse. He was rough on my sister and me, and we eventually developed the muscle necessary to withstand his attacks. My mom, on the other hand, never developed that muscle. She didn't have it in her. It would be like asking a bunny to be a tiger; it just wasn't possible. So I found myself standing up not just for myself but for my mom and even my sister at times. I actually worried that my mom would get hurt one day. In the end, my father never was physical with any of us, but it was so heavy and so much for me to deal with.

Over the years, I would ask my mom why she stayed. The biggest reason was love, but fear was a close second. Divorce still wasn't common and certainly wasn't accepted, and my mom had never really worked in a way that would make her feel confident about supporting herself and her children financially. Or emotionally, for that matter. She did reveal that she had thought about leaving at times, but even if she had decided to go that route, she just didn't have the confidence in herself. She didn't believe she could sustain a career, and she was such an overachiever and perfectionist that she would rather not try than try and make a mistake or fail. What an internal prison to live in!

Not surprisingly then, my mom would regularly tell me she admired my confidence, my strength and my belief in myself. She loved that about me, but she also envied it. It was something she wanted for herself, but she just couldn't get out of her own way, or around the family system she had set up, to go and get it. Ultimately she blamed herself, her insecurities and her fear of failure, as well as my dad because he needed her to be available in such a way that would never fully allow her to immerse herself into a career. That was just one more way his anger and dominance impacted of our lives.

TIPS & TAKEAWAYS

How to Manage Anger

Growing up in a home where anger was an everyday occurrence and outbursts were as normal as brushing your teeth, I had a front-row seat to anger's impact on both the perpetrator and the victims. As I grew up, anger became my language. It was my compass for "normal" relationships, whether they were romantic, platonic or familial. So the first time I was in a relationship where there was no anger, I didn't know what to do. There were no explosions, there was no drama, and that was completely outside my norm. I kept wondering what was wrong!

Now, of course, I won't settle for less. That's not to say that I don't have conflict in my relationships. It's just that I don't let anger serve as the overriding emotion. I am careful to watch my words so that I don't hurt others, and I am very clear in my communication so that I can avoid buildups that end in angry outbursts.

Here is how you can keep anger at bay as well:

1. **Pause**: When we are confronted with a strong emotion, we tend to respond with an equally strong emotion. Actually, we are not responding so much as we are reacting. So one of the keys to managing anger is learning not to react but to instead take the sacred pause. This proverbial timeout prevents you from being at the mercy of your emotions. It allows you to remain in control of your actions, and it gives you the space you need to decide what comes next, whether it's a strong reaction or waiting for your strong emotions to pass. This is not easy, but that's okay. We have a goal, and goals take hard work!

2. **Think before you speak**: In the heat of the moment, it is easy to say things you will regret. Always take a few

moments to gather your thoughts before you speak, and let others do the same.

3. **Get some exercise**: Burn off some of the emotion, and clear your head before responding. You can go to the gym or just take a short walk. Any physical movement helps.

4. **Identify possible solutions**: Instead of staying focused on what made you angry, work on potential solutions. Problem-solving is what will make things better.

CHAPTER 7

After two years in New York, my time at elementary school was drawing to a close. Seventh grade would mark yet another transition and, with it, another chance to grow into a better version of myself. This was such a valuable lesson for me: You can decide to reinvent yourself anytime you want to, but it's always easiest when there's a natural transition like starting a new school, going away to camp or being in between jobs. These little disruptions between one phase of life and the next give you time to grow and bring your best new self to the next endeavor. Opportunity is the mother of reinvention.

My middle school was on the Upper East Side, just a bus ride (which I had not been back on since the violations) across town. Socially, it was a good fit. I realized I could be a bit of a chameleon and change my colors to fit the situation in front of me. I got along with pretty much everyone, but I was still acting out, being reckless and taking risks that would ultimately hurt me as well as my family.

I went to my first nightclub when I was 13 years old. I told my parents I was going to see the movie *Platoon*, and when I came home an hour past curfew, they asked me about the movie. I didn't know that my parents had called the mother of the friend I had supposedly gone to the movie with. Nor did I know that my friend's mom had informed my parents that we had gone to a nightclub. So when my parents described a false summary of the movie, I just nodded my head. (In contrast, I can't even imagine my kids doing anything like that when they were 13. It shows me how solid and together my kids were at that age in contrast to the mess I was.) That night marked the beginning of my teenage rebellion. It was not a fun night, but it quickly became one of many. Similar to the apologies from my dad, I would apologize, promise not to do it again and then be somewhere I shouldn't be the very next weekend. I just did not care. It was as though I was completely tuned out and turned off. By the time I was completing eighth grade, I was a wreck. My parents and I had gotten into this vicious cycle where I could do no right. My response was to retreat into my own world and stop trying to get their approval, because I was never going to be able to meet their expectations anyway. I had no respect for my parents or our relationship. This was probably because I had no respect for myself and because so many boundaries were broken in my home life. I had grown to hate myself. Every time I would look in the mirror, I would see Dave. I would see a disgusting monster, and if a disgusting monster wanted me then I must be a disgusting monster too.

And so the disgusting behavior continued. I would routinely lie to my parents. They would find out, I would get in trouble and then I would do it all over again. I was young, and the party scene for teens was intense. I really don't know how I managed to avoid the drugs that were abundant at these parties, but I just knew that there was a line I was willing to get close to but not cross. I suppose it was that inner voice of mine as well as the support of my family, because as abusive and dysfunctional as my family life was, it was also loving and grounded.

That's why it was all so confusing. I was clearly screaming for help, but no one seemed to understand the cry. I had seen a variety of therapists by this time, and while everyone pointed to my dad and my family dynamics as an explanation for my behavior, as well as for my learning disability and impulsivity issues, those were just red herrings. They exacerbated my problems, but they were certainly not the primary cause. And up until that point, I had not been strong enough to tell anyone my secret.

One day, on our way to yet another professional who had been hired to "fix" me, I just decided to confide in my mom about the abuse. We were in a taxicab, and I remember the smell of my mom's perfume combined with the fragrance of her makeup that she had flawlessly applied. She always looked so sophisticated and put together, which only heightened the irony of her taking her broken daughter to see yet another specialist.

I dived right in. "Mom," I said, "I want to tell you something, but it's awkward and uncomfortable, and you have to promise not to tell anyone, okay? I'm not positive, and I don't want to get anyone in trouble, but I think I was sexually abused by Dave. I'm confused, because I know I lie and make up stories, so it's hard to know if I'm making this up or if it really happened."

I questioned my inner voice because of the stories that I'd had to create to escape my world. The lines between truth and reality had gotten so blurred that I could no longer trust what I thought was true.

All I wanted at that moment was for my mom to take me in her arms, hug me and tell me she believed me and that it was going to be okay. Instead, my mom sat there looking at me as if I had 10 heads. She agreed that it was probably hard to know given my history of making up stories, and she agreed there was no need to tell anyone.

What?! If anyone comes to you saying he or she might have been sexually abused, please believe that person. Whether or not it's as bad as you or that person might think, there is probably some grain of truth to it. At the very least, there is some issue there that needs to be addressed. My mom, for all her amazing attributes, was very, very skilled at sweeping things under the rug when they made her uncomfortable.

I reminded my mom not to tell anyone about this conversation, especially my dad, which was a request she unfortunately respected. (If you can call it respect. Sometimes I think it was more fear.) Funny how, out of all the secrets I asked her to keep from my dad, this was the one she chose not to share. Nor did she tell my therapist. What's worse, she offered me no guidance or tools to help me through the process. It was as though it was more important to her to keep it a secret more than it was for me!

In fairness to her, I did frame the abuse as a possibility rather than a certainty. And while I now know that, as the responsible adult, she had an obligation to tell both my dad and my therapist, I understand her perspective. In the years since that conversation, I learned that there had been sexual abuse in her family too, and the person who had abused me had probably been abused himself. I honestly believe she did the best she could at the time.

If my mom could have shared more about her family and background, the suffering I was forced to endure could have been seriously mitigated. But none of us, not even my dad, had any idea that this haunted her family. I guess she was too ashamed and, out of a misguided sense of loyalty to her family of origin, she made a choice to ignore my experience even to the detriment of my health and well-being.

It has been documented that victims who receive early intervention and treatment for sexual abuse wind up more successful in all areas of life than those who receive treatment later on or never. Years later, my mom and I talked through it, and she was so sorry for not being more protective. She admitted she had been scared, and I truly believe that my experience brought up some issues from her own past that she just wasn't ready to confront. My mom was my rock. She would drop anything at any time to be there for me. She just didn't always understand me, though I know in her heart she wanted to.

So, like those of many others, my childhood was an uphill battle for survival that was peppered with opportunities to thrive. Moving to New York allowed me to reinvent myself and start over. It also allowed me to enjoy a more fulfilling social life, although I still didn't catch certain cues the way I like to think I would have if I hadn't been so defeated by past events. I think I wanted social acceptance and normalcy too much, and when you want something as badly as I did, you often get in your own way. I would meet a guy or have some new girlfriends and instead of treating them well, I would become close to them and then do something to destroy the relationship. Classic intimacy issues, right? Talk about self-sabotaging! In eighth grade, for example, I had a best friend. She gave me one of those best-friend necklaces where you each wear half of the heart. One night, I called her and told her I was putting the necklace she had given me in the blender. I turned on the blender for her to hear and basically said we were no longer best friends. At the time, I felt like she was bothering me, and I thought it was cool to be mean. Looking back now, I understand the real reason was I was scared to get close to her.

I have since forgiven myself for that and similar experiences, but the forgiveness took time. And while I would do it differently now, I also know that, had it been easy for me back then, I wouldn't be who I am today. I wouldn't appreciate every single thing in my life, because I wouldn't know the other side of it. As my mom always reminded me, you bring yourself wherever you go. I didn't fully understand the impact of that statement at the time, but it slowly sank in until I realized that I had choices and could change the way I lived my life. Over time, that understanding has flourished. Now I am happy to take myself with me wherever I go. Choice is an amazing power to exercise should we choose to do so. Once I fully grasped that, things began to shift. But all that would come further down the road. I still had a lot of life to live first!

TIPS & TAKEAWAYS

Embrace Change and Reinvent Yourself

Throughout my life, I have had many occasions to reinvent myself. Until I became happy with who I was, I was constantly evolving, trying on different perspectives and attitudes to see what fit best. I would keep on one persona for a while until it was time to shed that skin and grow in a different direction. Initially, I resisted changing because it felt like doing so was an admission that I wasn't good enough. But as I started to make the changes (resistance and all), I could see the benefits. Each baby step of progress inspired me to keep trying and pushing through.

When you find yourself at a crossroads, whether it's a new job or a pattern of experiences you'd like to change, it's time to seek growth.

Here's where to begin:

1. **Get to know yourself and your strengths**: Reflect on what has worked for you and what has not. That will direct you to where your strengths lie. Ask friends, family and colleagues for feedback, and be sure to stay open, whether you agree or not. Once you have this information, it is easier to self-manage.

2. **Try out different things, attitudes and actions**: Experiment and have fun! We are creatures of habit, but breaking your habits and getting out of your comfort zone will allow you to have new experiences that enable you to explore what is possible. Maybe it's a trip someplace new or a different career – the idea is to learn about yourself and your potential. Some will be successes and others will be failures, but what is most important is that you aren't afraid to try.

3. **Be courageous**: Setbacks will happen. Sometimes what you want is more than you think you might deserve or be able to handle. (It's not.) Keep going and take ownership of

your innate power of choice. It is up to you to manage your emotions and keep pushing forward.

4. **Remind yourself of the commitment you made to yourself**: Fears and self-doubt are sure to appear when we embark on anything new, especially when it comes to our own selves. Make sure to manage these emotions so you don't get discouraged. Notice them and bring yourself back to center, back to the commitment you made to reinvent yourself.

5. **Accept failure, learn and resume your journey**: Failure is part of the process. Recognize it, learn from it and move on!

CHAPTER 8

So, there I was, living in New York City with every opportunity in front of me, and I still couldn't manage to get out of my own way. I was 13 years old and struggling to hold on. I remember thinking over and over, *I am at the bottom of this deep, dark hole. How am I going to climb out of here? How long will it take?* The ballast to these feelings was my inner strength. No matter how down I got, no matter how bad things were, I had that to fall back on. It was my guide to get me to where I am today.

My way out, however, came with a lot of detours. I would make progress only to find myself back at the bottom again, each time looking for a new way to claw my way into the light. I had access to every possible resource, yet my shame stopped me from moving forward. My mom's reaction to my abuse only reinforced that it should remain a secret, which underscored for me how shameful it must be.

In many ways, my feelings were textbook reactions. Children who are sexually abused keep it a secret because of the fear, the humiliation, the shame and a sense of responsibility. Abusers often convince children that they are the ones to blame for the abuse, so they will either be punished or not believed. Also, since there is frequently a preexisting relationship between the abuser and the victim, the victim does not want to betray the abuser.

My abuse, coupled with a difficult home life, left me unable to process things for myself. But even once I had those tools, nothing was going to change until I got honest with myself. I am here to tell you it has taken me more than 40 years, and while I am no longer climbing out, staying out is a choice that takes work. As with so many things, you can't just get to this point and expect to stay here. You have to work to stay afloat.

Perhaps you are in a similar situation. It might be an emotional struggle, an addiction, a negative mindset or an abusive relationship, physically or verbally. No matter what the cause, getting out is only half the battle. Staying out is the most important part. And while our experiences may differ in the details, I remember clearly the struggles of each phase of my life, and I can relate to what you are going through.

TIPS & TAKEAWAYS

Putting a Stop to Self-Sabotaging Behavior

For as long as I can remember, I was the queen of self-sabotaging behavior. Anything I could do to push people away, whether I was conscious of it or not, I did it. But no matter which self-destructive thing I did, the result was always the same: I would hate myself. Eventually, I got to the point where this vicious cycle had to end. It took me time and lots of deep, introspective work to realize that I was the cause of most of my issues. Maybe I wasn't the one who set the cycle in motion – I had my abuser to thank for that – but I was the one who chose how to act and react. Once I was able to see that the power was within me, I got to work.

The work took years to do. It took strength, it took painful moments, and it brought joyous ones. It was not easy, but was it worth it!

Here is where to begin:

1. **Understand self-sabotage**: Self-sabotage is when a part of your personality acts in conflict with other parts of your personality. Essentially, it is a resistance to the flow of life, and it almost always stems from deeply rooted feelings of inadequacy. Understanding what your self-sabotaging patterns are is a critical first step to breaking them. Without awareness, it is impossible to make intentional changes.

2. **Recognize self-sabotaging habits**: We all have different habits that undermine our goals and set up patterns for self-sabotaging behavior. Yours might be giving up on something before you even go for it. Your friend's might be maintaining harmful relationships. Get to know your self-sabotaging habits so you can begin to stop them before you enact them.

3. **Go inward to identify root causes**: Putting an end to your self-sabotaging patterns and habits is easier when you know why you started them in the first place. Explore what triggers you today and what has triggered you in the past. When was the first time you remember experiencing that feeling or habit? What caused it? What did it feel like?

4. **Exercise self-reflection**: Self-reflection is key to both personal growth and preventing self-sabotaging behavior. It takes a lot of self-reflection to understand why you keep getting in your own way. Taking the time to peel back the layers can offer insight into yourself and why you do the things you do. Start by having a conversation with yourself about an experience that left you feeling deflated. Usually we ignore these feelings or beat ourselves up over them. Instead, ask yourself why you did whatever it was that ultimately sabotaged your goals or experience. What came up for you that caused you to act that way? When have you felt that same way in the past? (See Tip No. 3.) The more you directly question these patterns, the sooner you can take your life in a new and healthier direction.

5. **Find the leader within**: We spend so much time listening to our inner critic and assuming that voice is right. When we recognize the areas in which we limit ourselves, however, we can start adjusting our behavior to find ways to tap into our inner leader. This voice serves as your champion and cheerleader, and it is the one to heed. As opposed to your inner saboteur!

6. **Make small but meaningful changes**: Make a list of everything you want to change, and pick one thing to be your starting point. Take baby steps, and build slowly on your success. The goal is not overnight transformation but consistent and sustainable change that eventually touches all parts of your life.

CHAPTER 9

Growing up in Manhattan in the '80s and '90s was definitely interesting. The city was being cleaned up, but things were still pretty gritty out there. Central Park, for example, was essentially off-limits to me. The adults in my parents' circle were focused on their own social lives, so that gave us kids a lot of freedom to go clubbing and drinking, host or crash house parties (yes, I hosted my share of them) and hit the bars. Fake IDs were easy to get and no one cared, so you could be 14 years old and enjoying the club life. At that time in my life, I was on track to get into some serious trouble. Entry to this world typically started around the time we turned 14. You can imagine how fun all of that may feel at 14, but the fact is few are mentally or emotionally equipped to handle the stimulation and situations that come along with such freedom. I pretty much had free rein, especially when I compare my adolescence to my own children's insulated suburban lives.

In some ways, though, that freedom was welcome and necessary for me. Between the abuse and my two controlling, Type A, overachieving parents, I needed some space and independence to rebel. And rebel I did! I honestly can't believe I survived, let alone become a well-adjusted woman with little baggage left to unpack. Although my parents' intentions were loving and solid, they just missed the mark a lot of the time. This was common among their generation. In fact, I give them credit for being more advanced, in some ways, than their peers. But the fact was I often found myself in precarious situations that were as scary and unpredictable as they were fun and exciting.

My parents, meanwhile, were loving life. My mom was drawn to anything that involved learning. She met life with abundant curiosity and found living in the suburbs to be oppressive. Moving to the city opened up a whole new world for her, and she flourished. She loved being able to go about her day, unfettered by no longer having to drive my sister and me around. She felt stimulated the moment she walked out of our apartment building: the people walking around, the architecture, the energy, the vibe. New York was buzzing, and she was a daily witness to it!

My dad was also in his element. His business was just starting to take off, and you could feel and see how that energized him. His sense of self-worth was always tied up with his professional success. My parents' excitement was contagious. They were working the circuit, from joining charitable organizations to attending galas and dinners at places like DANIEL, Tavern on the Green, Del Frisco's Grille, The Palm, Jean-Georges and Per Se. If you can imagine the TV show *Gossip Girl* without as much drama, then you can picture their life. Actually, scratch that. Their lives were *Gossip Girl* with the drama, just a different drama.

As my dad began to keep pace with the people he was associating with, we went from living a modest, middle-class life to having luxuries that I didn't even know existed. Rather than shopping at the flea markets as we did in New Jersey, for example, we began frequenting stores like Bergdorf Goodman, Ralph Lauren and Barneys. While that may seem glamorous, it was actually exhausting – I felt like I had to keep up an image that wasn't even mine.

My dad, always an addict at heart, now became addicted to his success, and his moods would allow us insight into what kind of day he had. When you hit a certain level of success, the pressure can sometimes make it feel like the walls are closing in on you. On those days, we knew to stay out of his way. At least I did. But that didn't always work, because he needed to unleash somewhere. Everywhere, actually, so my sister, my mom and I were often the targets of his frustration. We weren't the only ones though. There were also his friends, relatives, colleagues and employees, as well as servers at restaurants, cabdrivers and really any and all service professionals. In this, he did not discriminate. He would berate us and put us down, calling us names like "effing idiot" under his breath or telling us we were worthless.

It was hard for me to take but even harder for me to hear him do this to my mom. I decided that I had to become her voice. It was a quiet voice at first. I was so frustrated that she would let him talk to her like that, but I also knew she just didn't have the inner strength to fight him. This amazing woman devoted her whole life to him. She couldn't get a job or have a career of her own because he needed her to be at his beck and call. Not having her own career was one of her biggest regrets in life. She had always felt she wasn't good enough because she did not earn a living, but this was because of her situation with my dad, and I made sure she knew she was enough. Instead of my mom working and getting paid for her time, she gave her time and her heart so freely to all of her passions. She paid to do what she loved instead of getting paid. She changed lives because of who she was and how she interacted with people. And she did an enormous amount of philanthropic work while also donating an enormous amount of money. She was enough. She was more than enough!

It was a difficult position to be in and a difficult responsibility to bear, being a child who feels as though she needs to protect her parent. But that was the role I took on. I realize now that I have always protected my mom. Not just from my dad but also from the abuse and trauma I endured. Even now, when I look back on the day I told my mom about the abuse, her silence and fear triggered me into protecting her. That's why I immediately softened up my confession. It was to help her by letting her off the hook, even at the expense of my own feelings and needs.

As I began to feel and accept the truth of all that I had been through, there came a point when I could no longer protect my mom. I told her that I was sure the abuse had happened. I had no doubt, and in fact I was worried that Dave was still doing this to others. I wanted to meet with an attorney to make sure we stopped him. By that time, I am pretty sure my dad was aware of what had happened, but he and I wouldn't discuss it until much later. My mom and I met with a legal team, and they decided we had a case since we hadn't yet passed the statute of limitations. We met with the attorneys several times and even hired a private investigator, but in the end we decided not to pursue the case, at least not for the time being. I realized I wasn't ready; there were many steps of healing I needed to go through first. I was still at the beginning stages of processing the reality of all of it. How could I talk about this and advocate for myself and others when I was only just coming to terms with it? The case evaporated because, without any hard evidence, and without my being ready to testify, I couldn't take that next step. I knew I could be letting other victims down by not speaking up, but I just couldn't do it. I had to make my self-care the priority.

Life continued to be messy for me. I had yet to realize that I was the only one who could save me. Indeed, I would have to save myself more than once over the years to come. But every time I did, I would discover certain advantages: a new stage of life, a stronger sense of self-respect and, most importantly, my voice.

TIPS & TAKEAWAYS

Finding Your Voice

Finding your voice isn't always easy. We tend to get caught up in other people's voices, and those can sometimes influence us even more than our own. For me, I was fortunate that all the negativity surrounding my youth never truly silenced my inner voice. Sometimes it subdued it, but it never fully went away, and a part of me always knew well enough to trust it.

Here's how to find – and listen to – yours.

1. **Spend time alone**: Spending time alone can be exhilarating or scary, depending on your perspective, but it is always the best way to get to know yourself. Find out who you currently are as well as who you want to be. Ralph Waldo Emerson once said, "Nothing can bring you peace but yourself." Well, nothing but being alone can bring you a strong sense of identity. Don't be afraid to be alone!

2. **Listen**: Tune out the noise and tap into yourself so you can hear your voice. It is something that is best identified in stillness and silence when you are calm, centered, grounded and able to step away from any emotional turbulence you may be experiencing. From the stillness, answers emerge.

3. **Embrace the power of you**: Once you find/identify your voice, start using it! Whether in texts or calls, in casual conversations or meetings, take every opportunity to practice and embrace your authentic voice. When you embrace your own unique voice, not only can it alleviate fear and insecurity, but it also can open doors that you weren't even aware existed.

CHAPTER 10

I was getting ready to start ninth grade, and it would be my third year at the elite private school I attended. The unofficial acronym for my school, Dwight, was Dumb White Idiots Getting High Together, so while it was exclusive, it was on the lower end of the spectrum and nothing compared to the top college-prep school my sister attended. I was told repeatedly that there was no way I could handle a school like my sister's. While that was probably true thanks to all the "stuff" I was dealing with (and maybe I couldn't have hacked it even without all the emotional upheaval), I was made to feel slow and inadequate, as if something were wrong with me for attending a different school.

One day, I was in my bedroom thinking about school, and the prospect of another year felt so draining and depressing. I was desperate to get away – away from my life, away from my parents and their suffocating rules and expectations, away from the nightmare of Dave. The whole thing was crushing. I knew something needed to change with both my self-destructive behavior and my relationship with my parents. Soon, my thoughts turned to a few magazine articles I had read about boarding school. That, I decided, could be a solution.

I worried about leaving my sister and my mom with my dad, but I just couldn't survive in such a toxic environment anymore. I felt like I was dying a slow death, and I was no good to anyone. I guess this was only reinforcement that I had to take care of myself first. I couldn't rely on anyone to save me – that was my job – and I couldn't save anyone else until I saved myself. It had been almost five years since we had moved to Manhattan. I had grown so much by that point, and I realized there was yet another opportunity to reinvent myself.

So just a month before ninth grade began, I begged my parents to let me go to boarding school. I felt like it was my only chance at survival. I was already a sensitive empath who was scared and always on edge thanks to my dad's unpredictable moods. I felt like I was suffocating, and I just couldn't sustain that type of lifestyle. I was close to burnout.

Because my request came at the very last minute, there were not a lot of options for schools. I wound up in the middle of the Berkshires at a school that billed itself as mainstream but whose student population was decidedly not. While I personally liked a lot of the kids there, their problems were very different from mine, and it was not a good fit for me. By mid-semester, I knew that I had to leave the school. My inner voice was screaming that I was in the wrong environment. But was I really going to put my parents through another change?

One of the many gifts my dad gave to me was to trust in myself. Even though I had made up stories for most of my life and acted out in ways that understandably squandered other people's trust in me, my dad always, always believed in and encouraged my inner voice. That's why I would inevitably listen to it. It just came down to whether I would resist the voice before leaning in. As I got older and developed more confidence and comfort with myself, I would listen to that voice as soon as I heard it.

Back then, however, it took me a little while before I told my parents just how miserable I was. I said that I wanted to continue to go to boarding school (being away from the dysfunction of my home had been my saving grace) but that the school we had selected was not the right one. As much as it pained me to do this to my family and to myself, it would've hurt more to stay at the wrong school. At that age, you just want to find your place as best as you can for a few years. Thankfully, my parents understood. We found a new school that was legitimately mainstream with a beautiful campus and more traditional college-prep curriculum. I was ready for this new challenge, and I had one more valuable life lesson under my belt: There was powerful potential in using my voice to advocate for my well-being.

TIPS & TAKEAWAYS

Advocate for Yourself

I have always had a strong inner voice, and I have also always embraced change because for me, change has usually translated to an improvement on my current situation. But even after I figured out how to use my voice, I had to experiment with it in various situations so that I could truly and effectively advocate for myself.

When we moved to the city, my parents began to encourage my sister and me to fend for ourselves. Yes, they were present for us when we needed them, but they encouraged us to learn self-sufficiency, whether that was by making our own doctor and dentist appointments or conferring with our teachers when questions or problems arose. While I think this was a little premature, I will say that the payoff was I learned early on how to take care of myself at a very high level. I didn't need to depend on anyone for anything. So when something would come up for me, my first reaction was always to identify the best next step and how I could advocate for myself.

There are no handouts in this world, so if you want something to be different, you have to make it that way. That might require hard conversations with others, hard conversations with yourself and standing up for yourself even when it would be easier not to.

But if you don't advocate for yourself, who will?

1. **Believe in yourself**: This goes beyond paying lip service to your good qualities. What does this really look like? When you truly believe in yourself, you are aware of your strengths, you feel good about yourself, you know your value and you practice self-care.

2. **Get to know yourself**: In order to advocate for yourself, you need to know what you want, what your needs are, what you like and what you don't like. Without clarity on this, you'll find it nearly impossible to advocate for yourself.

3. **Plan a strategy**: When you're faced with a difficult situation, consider several ways to address the issue. With multiple options, you can formulate a plan that affords you the best opportunity for success. In the end, it's about getting what you need.

4. **Express yourself clearly**: When you get clear on what it is you want, be sure to be brief and stick to the point. Sometimes role-playing in advance with a trusted friend, family member or mentor can be helpful.

CHAPTER 11

My life had essentially consisted of me running away, over and over again, from anything good that came near me. Anything that included even a glimmer of intimacy or that might inspire personal growth. By the time I reached high school, I occasionally began to tap into what had always existed on a subconscious level: I didn't want to feel this way anymore. I consciously decided that I no longer wanted to participate in self-destructive behavior or in behavior that hurt other people. What's more, it began to dawn on me that I had some control over this.

I didn't know where to begin. I mean, I had done it all: I had lied, stolen, said hurtful things about people, hurt my parents and loved ones, and hurt myself in various ways. I had changed high schools; I would do the same in college, leaving as soon as things got too uncomfortable. I was constantly on the run. The only problem was that I was running from myself, and when you are running from yourself, there is truly nowhere to go. The only thing to do is change who you are and how you communicate with yourself.

I remember the pain and loneliness of those years, from the time the abuse started until my teen years, when I really began to wake up to who I was as a person. I remember the various ways that my traumas manifested themselves, from sucking my thumb well beyond the acceptable age, to biting my nails until they bled, to using food to manage my emotions, to shutting down when I was called on anything, to being constantly defensive, to ruining relationships, to suffering from insomnia. I just couldn't grab the reins and make the necessary changes.

Looking back now, I realize how much of my youth was spent searching for myself and who I was. I sought out experiences and relationships – my dog Rusty; skipping school; partying at clubs; going to boarding school – as a means of numbing my sadness and loneliness. I didn't realize it at the time, and was too young to know how to always do this in a healthy way, but I was essentially trying on different personas to find one that fit. I was trying to get to know me.

The cool thing was that, although my choices were not always what they would've hoped for, my parents usually listened to me, trusted me and supported each decision. Together, they had been through self-help programs like EST and The Landmark Forum, which allowed them to bring a philosophy and knowledge base to the family that encouraged introspection, evolution and mind expansion.

It perhaps speaks to the endless complexities of the human heart that my dad attended these courses. I think he began going as a way to support and join my mom, who had subscribed to progressive ways of thinking from an early age. Eventually though, my dad became an equal and active participant. He always wanted to be better than he was. He just couldn't always get out of his own way. In the end, my parents' open-mindedness benefited me tremendously. The practices and qualities they learned, like introspection and mind expansion, went a long way toward helping me survive. That said, my parents also had extremely high expectations. They were raised by Depression-era parents who loved them but only knew one way to parent: by the proverbial rod. This approach included constant belittlement and sometimes physical abuse: My dad endured regular beatings, many of them with a belt. The stories I have heard about both of their upbringings break my heart and help me to understand that, while they did better by their own children, they also brought with them plenty of baggage.

My parents shared a certain vision for their life, and my sister and I had supporting roles in that vision. The tacit message was always that we were meant to achieve the things my parents could not, thereby taking their accomplishments to the next level. While this stemmed from a desire for us to have what they deemed "the best," it came with an immense amount of pressure. Never mind that what they considered "the best" didn't necessarily align with my views. Living your best life, after all, isn't a one-size-fits-all kind of thing. It holds a different meaning for each person. As far as my parents were concerned, "the best" meant that my sister and I would excel academically, socially and philanthropically. We were to do this at the highest level possible; there was no room for error. This was difficult because, while I didn't know exactly what they were at the time, my goals, passions and desires were decidedly different from those of my parents. It was hard enough to tap into those as a teenager, let alone with the trauma I had experienced.

It just wasn't resonating with me. My parents were imposing their dreams on me and not letting me explore mine.

Even if my life plan had aligned with that of my parents, I would've still run into problems due to the scarcity mindset they had imparted to me. While my parents' mindset would evolve with time – as they became more secure, they also became generous philanthropists – the early mindset of scarcity was transferred to me. It wasn't until my teens and adulthood, as I did the self-development work of unpacking, processing and understanding my emotions and memories, that I was able to see the benefits of an abundant mindset. Such a mindset looks different for everyone. For me, it is about feeling the pain but not being a prisoner to it. It is about seeing the vast opportunities around me rather than what I might lack. It is about living a life that is as open and accepting as possible.

This work really began in my teens. It started small but, like a snowball, the cycle of introspection and change gathered momentum, eventually manifesting to the outside world as I grew older and advanced further.

Such work can be a life journey: If you are doing it right, it should never end. There are different levels of self-development and self-awareness to reach. There are times when you fall and get back up, always keeping faith that you can grow into the person you are meant to be despite the challenges that stand in front of you. I am grateful to have been able to pick up these tools and life skills despite the fact that they came with a lot of adversity.

If you are not getting the results you want in your life, that is when it is most important that you keep believing in this work of personal growth and you see it through rather than giving up and saying, "See? It doesn't work." No one is saying that it is easy. But when you release the desire for instant gratification, you let go of trying to control things you're not meant to control. You can control your reactions. You can exercise choice. The world around you is something you have to engage with and accept – or not.

The process is a lot like nature. You can see a pretty flower, pluck it and then, after a day or two, watch it wilt. Or you can do the work of nurturing a plant so that it takes root and thrives well into the future.

TIPS & TAKEAWAYS

Learn How to Communicate

For a long time, my communication skills were lacking, to put it mildly, because I didn't even know what I was feeling, and I didn't want people to see what was going on inside of me. I hid behind all sorts of masks, which protected me but also prevented me from being honest with myself and everyone around me. I didn't want anyone to really see me, and I avoided becoming attached to anyone. I also grew up in an environment where yelling and criticizing were the norm. It was only after we all worked on ourselves to become better people, gradually improving our relationships with each other as well, that that changed.

Healthy communication, both with oneself and with others, is a key component of personal growth. Because our communication skills affect everything we do, it's essential that we speak and interpret what we hear as accurately as possible.

Here's where to start:

1. **Listen more than you speak**: Be an engaged listener by not interrupting others while they speak and by paraphrasing what was said, which is an opportunity to clarify any confusing terms or potential miscommunication. It's best not to repeat the words verbatim but instead express the concept in your own terms. Effective ways of summarizing someone's words can include, "Let me see if I understand," or, "What I'm hearing is that…"

2. **Begin with empathy**: Empathy is powerful for many reasons – not just communication! Empathy means you understand what another person is feeling. When you grasp someone else's perspective and feelings, you can better comprehend what he or she is saying. You can also more effectively communicate your own ideas. Remember, this is not about kindness, sympathy or pity. It is about putting yourself in someone else's position, which in turn allows you to communicate in a way that is both resonant and powerful.

3. **Be willing to hear "no"**: Many of us view "no" as a form of rejection. However, when it comes to communication, allowing someone to say no without shutting down or retaliating demonstrates an important level of respect. This helps preserve the other person's emotional safety net while building trust and allowing the establishment of boundaries, all of which are part of effective communication.

4. **Pay attention to nonverbal cues**: Studies show that a good portion of communication is nonverbal. Don't forget that this goes both ways. Not only is it important to watch the other person's body language, but you have to be aware that your body is sending messages as well. The way you look, move and listen to another person reveals more than your words do about where you are and what you are feeling.

5. **Set an intention to connect**: Whether speaking one-on-one or to a crowd, it is important to remember that eye contact builds credibility, establishes a sense of connection and illustrates that you care about the people you are communicating with.

6. **Make sure you are clear about what you are trying to communicate**: Always know your why, and be intentional when communicating it. If you don't understand what you are trying to say, nobody else will either. Your success will largely depend on your ability to concisely and clearly convey your message.

7. **Don't react**: Always remain calm and focused. When you are stressed out or emotional, you are more likely to send confusing and off-putting messages and regress into unhealthy communication patterns, like yelling. Being overly emotional also increases the likelihood that you'll misread the other person. Make sure to pause, take a deep breath and calm down before continuing an emotionally charged conversation. If you can't get yourself together, it's perfectly fine to take a break and come back to the conversation later.

CHAPTER 12

B ack to my story! High school was, in some ways, just as bad as elementary and middle school. Although I had more friends and more freedom, and although I had started to work on myself, I was still as lost as ever when it came to making my way with this boulder of a secret on my shoulders. I was lonely, hurting and always looking to fill the void, regardless of what the consequences might be for me, for my family or for my friends. The problem was the void was so deep and insatiable that nothing was going to fill it. It didn't matter how many schools I tried or how many friends I made. These things might change the backdrop to my life, but the suffering remained.

My second boarding school was beautiful and about an hour and a half from my home, which was nice. It was close enough that I could go home if I wanted to, but far enough away that I felt zero pressure to do so. The collegiate-like campus was leafy and idyllic, and while I still didn't feel like I fit in, I knew I would finish high school there. I made some nice friends who, thanks to technology, I am still in touch with today, but my old, self-sabotaging habits persisted back then. I pretty much created issues wherever I went and with whomever I became close to, all in an effort to avoid intimacy. Drama among friends wasn't my only symptom, though. For as long as I can remember, I have struggled with stomach and digestive issues. My stomach has always been where I hold all of my trauma, anxiety and emotions. I am not alone, of course. Today, there's plenty of research and dialogue around the enteric nervous system. Commonly referred to as "the second brain," the gut communicates regularly and profoundly with the central nervous system, providing clues about our emotional state. But back then, the connection wasn't widely known. All I knew was that I had frequent stomachaches.

One night, it was late and past curfew, and I was in my dorm room doubled over with stomach pain that was so bad, I ended up in the emergency room. I was told an internal cyst had burst. But why did I have a cyst, and why did it burst? Instead of focusing on finding a diagnosis (it turns out I had an autoimmune disease that remained undiagnosed for some time), my parents turned their attention in a different direction.

The stomach issues that plagued me when I was younger have stayed with me for most of my life and impact me even today. The difference is that now I know how to manage them. When I was younger, I tried to solve my ailments in a multitude of ways, but I just always seemed to feel best when I didn't have food in my body. That, of course, led me down a very dangerous road where I would restrict my food intake for days.

Food had always played a very big role in my family. A lot of our activities, family gatherings, trips and holidays revolved around food, which was a source of comfort and bonding. But my family also had plenty of issues around food, from overeating to constant dieting. So many extremes laid the groundwork for my own issues with food.

My parents were at their wits' end again by the time I was 16 years old, and they decided to admit me to an inpatient treatment facility with the hope of making everything better. My eating issues were the impetus for them to seek help, but we all knew it was so much more than that. I was struggling, I was miserable, I was still acting out and things were not good. I was dying inside, and we – me most of all – wanted it to be better. This is why my parents convinced themselves that the treatment facility was the answer. The doctors and specialists that my parents consulted with explained that my eating issues, which ranged from restriction to bingeing, were my way of exerting control within my chaotic world.

If they only knew! I didn't want to be struggling, but despite my best efforts, I wasn't equipped to fix myself. If it wasn't one issue, it would be another. I was going to keep acting out until I truly got a handle on myself, on who I was, on what I was dealing with and, most importantly, on who I wanted to be. I needed to address the real issue, but doing that was nearly impossible when no one, including myself, wanted to acknowledge that it even existed.

Being in the facility was surreal. How, I wondered, did we get to the point where I was in this place surrounded by these other damaged and broken teenagers? Did I really belong here? In my typical form, I decided to make the best of the situation. I became friends with a girl named Tina. She was clearly the leader and had been there for quite a while. At the time, her boyfriend was a well-known rapper. She and I couldn't have been more different yet, in the setting we were in, it didn't matter. Everyone knew not to mess with Tina, and since she and I were tight, it meant you didn't mess with me either. I made lots of friends, met a guy and had an escape from real life. It was definitely a motley crew, but it was my motley crew.

The only truly difficult times in the facility were when we had family therapy. My parents would come out to the facility for weekly sessions, and we would primarily talk about the dynamic between my dad and everyone else. Unfortunately, we never once spoke of the abuse. One thing that did come out of those sessions was that my mom should not try to protect me or my sister from our dad. Instead, she was advised to let us figure things out for ourselves. In a normal situation, this might have been sound advice, but our situation was complicated. And while my mom wasn't capable of protecting us, the therapist telling her to stay out of it just gave her even more permission to let us fend for ourselves.

The facility wasn't horrible, especially since my friends and I were always breaking the rules and finding ways to have fun. The only times that it got really bad (aside from family therapy) were when I was alone at night in my bed. The room was pretty nondescript with two beds (I had a roommate); a gross, brown carpet; two side tables; and a small bathroom. We were on the first floor. During the days, I loved being on the ground level, because I would dream of ways to escape through the windows. But at night, fear overcame me. I was petrified that an intruder would come through one of the windows or that one of the doctors, nurses, therapists or staff members would come in and violate me. Ironically, the facility that was supposed to help and support me in overcoming my demons and fears was, in this way at least, just perpetuating them!

After about four to six weeks, I was discharged. By that point, I had learned the script and knew what to say to get the doctors and therapists to sign off on my recovery. I had mentioned to my primary therapist at the facility that I thought something may have happened to me when I was younger, that a relative may have abused me. But instead of following up on that, the therapist latched on to my family issues and never mentioned the abuse with me, the family therapist or anyone else. This was yet another person who dropped the ball. The message was loud and clear: No one wanted to touch the abuse.

TIPS & TAKEAWAYS

Listen to Your Body

Our bodies and minds are designed as one symbiotic unit, and awareness is the key to making the mind-body connection. Our body listens to our mind, and our mind listens to our body. Every cell knows when we are unhappy and anxious just as every cell knows when we are happy and joyful. It's up to us to tune in so that we can be in touch with ourselves on a deeper level.

My body has always talked to me through my stomach. When I was a young child, it was with regular stomachaches. As I got older, it was with infections, weight fluctuations and ruptured cysts. Throughout all the emotional upheaval, my stomach was guiding me. It wasn't until I recognized the connection, however, that I could listen to the subtle cues or the loud screams telling me that things needed to change. Of course, changing my diet and exercise helped, but it was the mind-body connection that allowed me to "meet" myself and begin to heal both physically and mentally.

Bringing awareness to yourself is the gateway to vibrating at a higher frequency. Without self-awareness, it is nearly impossible to change your frequency. When you bring awareness to yourself, what you let into your mind, the food you let into your body, the movement you do, the self-care you practice and the people you surround yourself with all literally impact your vibrations at a cellular level. Vibrations and frequency are about energy and raising your own energy. As you start to do more of what raises your energy, including positive thinking and the things mentioned above, you will attract more of that into your life, because what you are focused on expands. So if you want more good in your life, practice gratitude; if you want more love in your life, be more loving; and so on. When you become more self-aware, you expand your consciousness and naturally feel lighter in your physical, mental and emotional body. You start to glow from the inside out. Trust me – once you start to feel this way, you will never want to go back to lower-vibration living.

1. **Feel what you feel**: We are often so busy ignoring or denying what we feel that it's no wonder our emotions find other outlets. When you get in an argument, when someone cuts you off in the car, you have a physical reaction that signals an emotional state. You might try to deny or distract or numb yourself from it, but this never works in the long term. Keep your attention on the sensations in your body

until they pass. Before you react with your head, pause and check in with your heart.

2. **Take a few deep breaths**: Breathing deeply and slowly allows you to ground yourself, refocus and come back to center. If you have a reaction you don't like, take a moment to be with the feelings, to let them wash over you. Then, take a breath to retrain your mind and your cells to react differently.

3. **Ask your body questions**: Check in with your body, and notice how you're feeling. Then, dig a little deeper to find out what's going on. Why, for example, do you have butterflies in your stomach? Is it nerves, excitement or anxiety? Why do you have a headache? Maybe you are dehydrated or simply need to stretch. Once you pay attention to how and what you are feeling, you can respond accordingly. Awareness is key.

4. **Listen**: Our bodies talk to us all the time. Do you feel a sense of ease, lightness, energy, abundance or high vibrations? Do you have stomachaches, headaches or sore muscles? Pay attention. The good feelings indicate when your life and body are in alignment. They encourage you to do more of what you are doing so you can live in that space. Alternately, the bad feelings are trying to prompt you to make necessary changes in your life. Tune in!

5. **Trust the answer**: Your body never lies. Once you start to listen and practice more self-awareness, you can begin to trust the answers that your body gives you. From there, you can make positive and necessary changes.

CHAPTER 13

As I neared the end of high school, some things started to work out while other things continued to unravel. This wasn't surprising. I was approaching another transition out of high school and into college. Naturally, everything in my life would shift. Naturally, I would reinvent myself.

When I was 17 years old, the digestive issues that were a chronic source of discomfort for me, and which had landed me in a treatment facility, really flared up. I was bloated and inflamed, and I suffered from migraines as well as joint issues. I had always been unwell to some degree, but this was different. My mom took me to a variety of specialists, but no one was able to provide a diagnosis. Everyone believed it was an autoimmune issue, but the tests were inconclusive. Nevertheless, I was put on a number of different antibiotics that caused me to swell up, lose my hair and feel fidgety and nervous. All these side effects came with zero benefit: I wasn't cured; in fact, I'd never felt worse.

This was definitely not the way I wanted to spend senior year. At some point, we accepted that the meds weren't working, and a family friend introduced me to Dr. Leo Galland. I'd like to say he was our last hope, but we didn't know he would prove to be the miracle worker he was. He impacted my life in ways he probably isn't even aware of! This was 1991, and Dr. Galland, who specialized in complex chronic disorders, was considered an alternative doctor (now commonly referred to as a functional doctor). He followed a natural and holistic protocol, despite being a medical doctor who graduated from Harvard University and NYU Medical School.

My time with him predated his many awards (including a lifetime-achievement award and a ranking among the country's top doctors), but his then-groundbreaking approach felt intuitive and effective. In his view, the doctor-patient relationship should be a partnership that empowers people to take control of their own health.

Dr. Galland grounded his practice in three principles:

1. Search for the root causes of each person's illness; don't just suppress symptoms with drugs.
2. Treat every patient and every illness as unique.
3. Whenever possible, choose treatments that enhance rather than suppress normal functions.

Accordingly, Dr. Galland helped me from both a medical perspective and a lifestyle perspective. One of the first things that I had to do as part of my protocol was an elimination diet. While this is relatively popular now, it was unheard of then, and the options for gluten-free, wheat-free, yeast-free and dairy-free foods were both limited and unpalatable. It was hard being so restrictive, especially at my age when a lot of my social activities involved going out with friends for meals. Pizza and diner food, those staples of the teenage diet, weren't options for me with the protocol I was following. But I complied, and I started to feel better almost immediately. While there were many things that I missed, there was nothing I missed as much as feeling well. In addition to changing my diet, Dr. Galland had me add in supplements, receive acupuncture and make a variety of other lifestyle changes that enhanced my day-to-day life. I followed everything religiously for the first year or so until I was feeling well again, and then I loosened the reins a bit. While I did not always follow his guidelines as rigorously as I did in the beginning,

I had the tools I needed to readjust my habits any time my health began to decline, which would happen many times throughout the years. This was a game changer for me, and it was instrumental to the beginning of my health and wellness journey.

While my health began to get back on track during my senior year of high school, my approach to the rest of my life continued to feel messy. Specifically, I was not ready mentally or physically for the next step in life: college.

The fact that I can't remember any part of the application process or SAT testing reflects how hard and chaotic that time was. I was still struggling to fit in, struggling to accept myself, struggling academically, struggling with life.

Most Fridays, I would grab the train to Penn Station, sometimes with friends from school, sometimes alone to meet friends from home. My parents were rarely there as they liked to head out of the city on the weekends, and my sister was away at college, so my friends and I had the run of the apartment. We definitely used it to our advantage! It was a fun time but also, looking back, it was a dangerous time with us running around the city as if we owned it. Senior year ended, and I had gotten into several schools that I had applied to. To be honest, I have no idea how I even got into those schools. My grades were subpar at best, my SAT scores were embarrassing and I can't even remember writing an essay for the applications. I decided to attend a nearby university that was about five hours away. The school was in an urban environment with approximately 35,000 undergraduate students. Since it would be a big adjustment, my parents thought it would be a good idea for me to participate in a summer program designed to ease the transition for incoming freshmen. The program was several weeks long, and we would stay in a dorm, have roommates, etc., so that we could get the full "college experience."

It started off strong but also confusing. On my first day, I met some awesome people and we became fast friends. But I still didn't feel like I deserved "real" friends, and I continued to undermine myself by choosing toxic people and relationships. That was what I was used to and what I felt safe with. I was getting a lot of attention from guys, but anything that wasn't superficial made me extremely uncomfortable. Intimacy terrified me.

My friends and I would study by day and party at night. Despite having been part of the party scene for so long, it was never my scene. I found it hard to keep up with the social aspect, the partying, the school and feeling good. I also began to fall back into my old self-destructive and hurtful behavioral patterns, including drinking, skipping classes and eating badly.

It wasn't long before my body started talking to me: I felt scared and sick to my stomach all the time, knowing deep down that this was not the right place for me, that I could never keep up and that this wasn't going to work. Good times! So, yet again, I had to go home and tell my parents that I wanted to change schools. They weren't thrilled, but they supported me. We had about four weeks to figure out where I would go, and I decided on a school that was just an hour away. While it was not Ivy League, it was a great launching pad for me. I know my parents had higher hopes, and maybe it was difficult for them to tell their friends where I was at school, but regardless of image and name, it was the best next step for me.

I flourished at this school. I got a 4.0 and had a very significant relationship with a man who was so right for me at the time. We met on the first day and didn't leave each other's side the entire time we were there. I think it is fair to say that he was my first love. I also had lots of friends who were down to earth and who made me feel like I could be myself (whoever that was at the time). As the year progressed, I realized that, as great as the school and year had been for me, I was outgrowing it. The experience had given me a lot of confidence and a great foundation. Now I was ready for something more. So, yet again, I sat down with my parents. This time, though, I felt better about it because instead of a downward or lateral move, I was looking for something better. I wanted to level up!

My parents were cautiously optimistic and supportive and agreed it would be a good idea. The hardest part was leaving my boyfriend when our relationship was thriving. So, he decided to transfer too, although he stayed local while I settled on a school that was not as close and where I would not have the safety net of home. (Eventually my boyfriend and I went our separate ways, but we ended things on good terms. While we were serious at the time and our families had become close, we were too young and too far apart to make it work.) I started my sophomore year at Ithaca College. It was a solid school, not a top Ivy like my sister's and not even a tier below that, but it was better than where I had been, and the academics were more challenging. I made friends immediately, like I always do. (The challenge for me was never making friends. It was keeping them and not sabotaging the relationship.) The thing was, although I made friends easily, I never felt like I belonged. Whether it was my perception or the reality, I always felt like I was on the outside. What people saw didn't line up with who I was on the inside. This wouldn't change until much later in life when I began to work more on myself and less on fitting in.

As time went on, I became more and more unhappy. I wasn't feeling well physically and may have been depressed, so guess what happened next. Yup! You got it – it was time for a change. But what would that look like? I wanted to go home. I wanted to be away from the small mindedness and the toxicity that I found in the people and even myself while I was at Ithaca. I wanted to get away from the endless partying and the nights out that were such a blur, I could barely remember them. But then I wondered if I was just in the habit of running away from things. So I decided to carry on until maybe six months later when I just couldn't do it anymore! So I again had that conversation with my parents.

What, I wondered, was wrong with me, and why did I always have to be so difficult? What I would later come to understand is that I was neither difficult nor deficient. While many people do succeed in the situations that didn't work for me, there are just as many out there who follow a different path the way I did. Either they understand and accept that right away, or, like I did, they feel trapped, alone, different and almost like an imposter.

Thankfully, my parents understood. In fact, on some level, they were happy to have me come back so I could focus on my health. I transferred to New York University at the start of my junior year.

One advantage that moving around gave me was that each school I attended wound up being "better" than the last. NYU is pretty coveted and hard to get into. So while I was constantly changing, maybe I wasn't running away from things so much as I was running toward experiences where I could grow. Each step forward allowed me to shed personas and behaviors that didn't work for me so that I could eventually be who I was meant to be – my authentic self.

Life back in the city felt right. I definitely did not want a roommate and, at this point, I did not even want to live in the dorms. I wasn't transferring again for the typical college experience. Instead, I wanted to get my work done and get a job. I got an apartment not far from where I had grown up, and though there were times when I was lonely (everyone I knew was living a more conventional college experience), I knew this was best for me. Of course, being back in the city meant more time with my parents, which had its upsides and downsides. The upside was that I got along with them great, especially my mom, and spending time together was special. The downside was that I couldn't grow and figure out who I was when I was spending so much time listening to who they thought I should be, what they thought was best for me and what they wanted for me. Ours was a very codependent relationship, and extracting myself from that aspect of the relationship would prove to be very difficult.

TIPS & TAKEAWAYS

Go at Your Own Speed

Following your own path is a life lesson that has resonated with me since I was young. And I have only gotten more comfortable with it later in life. When I was 17 and my sister was at an Ivy League college, there were definitely moments when I felt pressure to follow her example, but I always managed to stay true to what worked for me, whether it was school or my social life. Eventually, I stopped looking at what everyone else was doing. When that happened, life changed for me. Everything changed. It didn't mean that everything was always good, but I was good. I was so stable and comfortable with myself that I knew I could handle anything. The trick is not to wait for your fear to disappear but to know intuitively when you're ready to get outside your comfort zone. Real growth happens when you start making decisions for yourself.

For me, I continued on my path of learning and getting to know myself at my own pace. While that meant and still means that I am different from many of the people around me, the payoff is that I am happy and I love my life.

Ready to march to the beat of your own drummer? Here's how:

1. **Check in with yourself on physical, mental and emotional levels**: The more self-aware you are, the more you can tune in to how you are feeling. And trust me, if you are not in alignment, your body will let you know. So pay attention!
2. **Don't compare your journey with anyone else's**: We are all on our own path, and comparing yours to that of your sister or your cousin or the guy in the corner office at work won't help you. It doesn't matter if you come out ahead or behind in such comparison. Just looking outward is a waste of time that distracts you from your purpose and path.

3. **The same thing doesn't work for everyone**: The other reason comparing paths doesn't work? The milestones along the way don't align for everyone. Say, for example, that your best friend is getting married at 25. His parents are thrilled. His fiancée is thrilled. He's thrilled. It does not, however, mean that you have to get married too. Your life must follow its own trajectory. You can try to force the course, but no matter how many detours you take because "it's time" to get married or land a job or have kids, life has a funny way of rerouting you on the path you're meant to take. Don't fight it. Embrace it. Life is not a one-size-fits-all.

4. **Do it for yourself and no one else**: You are not going to learn anything if you do it for someone else. There won't be any growth or passion because you are not doing it authentically. There's nothing wrong with saying to yourself, "No, I am not ready, but one day I might be," and work on getting there in your own time.

CHAPTER 14

I always wanted to be like my mom. She was a traditional homemaker in a lot of ways but also not. She could've lived a life of leisure, but she actively chose to fill the windows around caring for her family with meaningful work. She served on several philanthropic boards, but she also actively volunteered in a roll-up-your-sleeves kind of way. She was curious, radiant, sophisticated and committed to giving to others, whether it was to her family or to strangers she'd never meet. And, more importantly, she was the only person who would always, always, *always* be there for me no matter how ugly I became as a person, and no matter how many times I hit rock bottom. (My dad was there for me, too, but my mom offered far more empathy and patience.) Sometimes she was there in ways I didn't want her to be, and sometimes she wasn't there in the ways I needed her to be, but she was always there.

This isn't to say that she was perfect. She could be rigid and judgmental. She believed that her choices and decisions were the only right ones and that people who did not succeed, in whatever way that meant to her, failed because they didn't work hard enough or make the "right" choices. Because I looked up to her, that is what I was taught to believe as well, and I never questioned it until much later on. My mom seemed to have it together, and I wanted that too.

Naturally, then, I followed her example. (Never mind that her model was out of alignment with who I was.) That, combined with my dad's emotional abuse and alcoholism, and the mind games that sexual abuse plays with one's head, led me to seek validation through men. Male interest and approval were what made me feel best, even though (or maybe especially because) my self-esteem was at an all-time low. As soon as I got the attention I craved, and before there was any real physical or emotional intimacy, I would move on to the next one.

I avoided any risk of emotional attachment regardless of how the other person felt. It was a vicious, self-destructive cycle that wasn't fair to myself or the other person involved. That all changed one day, though. I was a senior in college, and I was invited to stop by a birthday party for my sister's friend. It was being held at a restaurant near my apartment, and I arrived toward the end of dinner. I was only planning on staying for a few minutes, but as I was mingling, someone stood up and offered me his seat. I looked at him and felt something I had never felt before – a sense of comfort. I stayed for a bit and made small talk with him. Eventually, I went home, but I made plans to rejoin the group later on that night at a bar. On my walk home, that inner voice chimed in again, and I just knew: I had met the man I was going to marry. I even called a good friend that night to say so!

We will call him Brian, and he was everything I wanted: funny, charming, charismatic and interested in me! He saved me in so many important ways, and I will always love him for that. I was just 22 years old when we met (he was 26), and while I didn't realize it at the time, he ultimately saved me from myself. He came into my life at a point when I had been partying regularly and interacting with people who left me feeling worse off than before I met them. On top of that, I was struggling with my identity, my self-esteem and my purpose. And perhaps most importantly, I was still heavily dependent on my parents for emotional support.

Before I met Brian, I needed constant approval and reassurance from my parents in order to feel comfortable moving forward with any decision. I thought they knew better than I did what was right for me. But as I started to feel safe with someone else, I began to trust myself more and this, in turn, allowed me to grow out of that childhood role and into a life that was true to myself. This was beyond liberating.

My parents only ever had the very best intentions, but their parenting was all tied up with their history, values, insecurities, opinions and expectations. While they were undoubtedly progressive in many respects, they were also very set in their ways. I could live my path with their full support so long as that path was within the box they had established. The message was subtle but clear: You are a reflection of your family, and how you behave represents us. This theme pervaded every aspect of my life. Forget about all the acting out I was doing. Forget about my dad's emotionally abusive tirades. No matter what was happening, no matter what we were feeling, once we set foot outside our home, we were expected to flip a switch and be a perfect, happy family. We had to swallow it.

With that firmly in mind, it was very hard to be true to myself while making sure to represent my family the way that I was supposed to! So I skipped out on so many things that I would have liked to experience, including starting fresh someplace else like Seattle or California. Out of fear, out of my limiting beliefs, I bowed to my parents' judgment and expectations.

Along the way, I definitely wished that it could've been different, that it could've been easier. And there were certainly times that I blamed my parents or society. But the truth was I always had a choice. I knew my parents, like anyone else, were limited beings doing the best they could, and I chose them. For a long time, I chose them. When I was ready, I moved on.

Anyway, back to my new and exciting relationship! By the time I met Brian, I had already had a couple of long-term relationships (I was a serial monogamist), but this was different. I loved how it felt to be with him, and I made the decision to commit to it. From the beginning, he and I became inseparable in a way that I needed so badly. I had been waiting for this moment my whole life, the moment when I would find the person who would complete me and love me in a way that filled me up. I had been waiting for the person with whom I would spend the rest of my life, with whom I would have children. My lifelong dream up to that point was to be a wife and have four biological kids and four adopted kids. (I wound up having three of the most amazing kids one could ever imagine.) I had been waiting for the person who would build that white picket fence with me, who would please my parents and society and who would enable me to pretty much live the way my mom appeared to the outside world.

I now know a different truth. I know that the only person who can love me in a way that completes me is…me. How empowering is that? It is within our own control! When that sunk in, and I went to the next level with it, it was intense. I learned that I didn't have to look for external sources to fulfill me, only to complement and enhance me. Looking outside ourselves for approval or to fill a void will never work out. We have to work on ourselves and come to relationships as a whole person who can give as much as we receive. That being said, I was 22, and my entire model for living life had been predicated on a traditional foundation embodied by the woman I admired most in all the world: my mom. It was a model that worked for her and which I made my own to a certain extent by graduating college, getting my master's degree and getting a job before settling down. For my mom, getting married meant staying home to take care of her husband and family. For me, well, things would turn out a little differently.

TIPS & TAKEAWAYS

Live Authentically

> "Be yourself – not your idea of what you think somebody else's idea of yourself should be."
> – Henry David Thoreau

Finding one's true self is a process for most of us, myself included. When I was younger, I spent a lot of time trying on different personalities in my search for myself. Sometimes this caused chaos around me, sometimes it inspired backlash, but I kept at it. There were also times when I assumed certain characteristics to fit in with a group of friends and see if that "worked" for who I was. This wouldn't change until much later in life when I began to work more on myself and less on fitting in. But once I made that shift, I discovered a world of freedom. Yes, my social circle was smaller, but there is nothing better than living as your authentic self, regardless of what anyone else says or thinks.

1. **Being yourself is not about standing out**: Being yourself is about following your own path, not comparing yourself to others. If you stand out as a result, that's great! But if your goal is to stand out, then you are likely compromising your authenticity and are instead checking the boxes of what you think will get you where you think you want to be. All that really gets you is a life unlived!

2. **Stay true to what you believe**: While it can be challenging in the short term, staying true to yourself and your beliefs ultimately brings you to a life of alignment, synchronicity and high vibration. Isn't that what we all want after all?!

3. **Be brave**: When you are courageous enough to express your genuine thoughts and opinions regardless of what others might think or say, you will experience a whole new level of acceptance and love for yourself. That, in turn, takes you to a whole new level of freedom. Enjoy!

CHAPTER 15

L ife isn't always the way it appears on the outside. Growing up, when we would hear stories of people in our circle who got divorced or were maybe on the brink of it, it was assumed that there must something wrong with them. That didn't exist in our family!

In reality, that wasn't so. I just couldn't see it then, because I was too busy judging everyone else. There was so much judgment in my family, which is sad. Now I recognize judgmental attitudes as a symptom of insecurity. I am not saying that I never judge, because I know I do. But I do my best to minimize my judgments and, more importantly, notice when I'm judging and remind myself that's not what I want to be doing.

There are so many ways to experience life. Who are we to pass judgment on any of them? I wish I had been more open at an earlier stage, because I missed out on getting to know so many amazing people as a result of those preconceptions. My family never really discussed what love truly is or how falling into societal traps can lead to a wake-up call that is simultaneously devastating and enlightening.

My mom and I had been so close all of my life. As I have said, I pretty much wanted to be her, and I just assumed that her path was my path. Not because of anything my parents explicitly said or did but because that was what was modeled for me. If only I had realized then that following their example was either going to make me very unhappy or give me a lot of unraveling to do later. Just because it was their path didn't necessarily mean it was mine!

Not only was I a different person living in a different time, but my circumstances were different too. Because of the sexual abuse, my dad's erratic behavior and my mom's desire to always please my dad, my self-esteem was, at that time, directly tied up with what guys thought of me. Typical daddy issues! So once I met Brian, I was euphoric! Life was magical! I felt free, supported and loved, and with all those feelings swirling around, I wasn't able to see that the relationship couldn't sustain itself. It never stood a chance. We were too young and inexperienced, just shells of ourselves. In retrospect, the amount of growth that would occur for me between the ages of 22 and 32 was impossible even to comprehend let alone predict.

As my relationship with Brian became more serious and headed in the direction of marriage, we started, ironically, to have more arguments, less communication and more distance. The thing was, I was convinced that what I had found felt right (whatever "right" meant) so I overlooked the signs. Perhaps more tellingly, all that conflict was subconsciously reassuring. The marital model I grew up with included a lot of tension, fighting, drama and conflict, so I just assumed that all that came with the territory. I think so many others think that as well, but it couldn't be further from the truth. When we start to work on ourselves and heal, we show up better, thus making our relationships better. Isn't that something that both we and our partners deserve? But this takes hard work and commitment, and sometimes it is easier for us to go on cruise control than it is for us to do the work.

It's easy to say with hindsight that Brian and I should have broken up way before we got married, but truth be told, I never would have wanted that. Brian was the first major external influence and catalyst for change that appeared in my life, and I am forever grateful for him. He was an all-around great guy, and he loved and balanced me in a way that I desperately needed. And probably in a way he desperately needed as well. He was solid next to my bundle of nerves; he made me feel safe, accepted, understood, protected and beautiful. He loved me when I was still not ready or able to love myself. Together, we made a strong team. Most importantly, he provided me with the best things ever to happen in my life: my children.

We unofficially moved into my apartment just weeks after meeting and officially moved in together about six months later. It was a wonderful relationship filled with lots of laughter, great times with friends and family, lots of growth and the building of a foundation for a future together. Family was also a huge part of our relationship. We spent every Christmas in the Midwest with his family and every Thanksgiving with mine watching the parade with friends and family from the comfort of my parents' apartment. Because we lived near my family, Brian became an integral part of our family dynamic. My dad finally had the son he had always dreamed of! We were young and in love and just enjoying the moment. Everyone around us fed off the energy and supported our new relationship. Finally, everything seemed to be flowing. Finally, I felt like I had direction. Not only was I falling in love with Brian, but I was also falling in love with my life. I could take a deep breath!

TIPS & TAKEAWAYS

Come From Curiosity

It wasn't until I was in my mid-20s that I realized there was judgment all around me. Though most of it was unintentional and unconscious, that didn't minimize or excuse its impact. Not only did it negatively affect my self-esteem and my view of who I should be, but it also rubbed off on me. I realized I was full of judgment too. I judged others, but I also judged myself, and I was my harshest critic. It wasn't until I started really connecting with myself that I was able to understand what was happening and why.

Once I was able to start witnessing my own behavior, I was able to adjust it. To me, judgment comes from a place of fear; a close-minded place. It stems from insecurity about how we feel about ourselves. I believe that, rather than judging, we should become curious. Curious about ourselves, our environment and others. I now find myself curious all the time. I love learning about myself and others. I want to analyze and learn and discover but not judge, so I always try to understand first.

Here is the process I follow:

1. **Adopt a curious mindset**: Curiosity supports open-mindedness and expansion, which allows us to freely explore new ways of thinking and being. It offers new ways to look at life.
2. **Notice when you judge**: Observing your judgments is the first step to and a critical part of releasing them. If we don't see them, then we can't shift from judgment to curiosity.
3. **Start a conversation with yourself**: When you notice you are feeling judgmental or out of alignment in any way, talk yourself through it. Ask yourself why you are judging or why you are having certain reactions, and try to get to the root of it. This will be an ongoing practice, but as you continue with it, you will notice your judgments gradually dissipate.
4. **Strive to understand**: Try to understand where the other person is coming from. We are self-centered beings by nature, but if we can find a way to remove ourselves, our emotions and our triggers from a given situation, we have taken the first step toward understanding. Everyone comes from a different set of circumstances, which will affect their view on things. All of it is directly related to that person's specific journey, not yours. If you can put yourself in the other person's shoes, it will help you judge less and understand more.
5. **Love**: Find love in your heart for yourself and everyone around you.

CHAPTER 16

And...the skeleton in the closet emerges!

It was 1997, and since my sister and I were no longer living with our parents, they decided that they were going to remodel our bedrooms into a single living space. This meant that it was time for us to go through the belongings that we had left in our rooms. So one afternoon, following a quiet morning in Central Park with Brian, he and I walked over to my parents' apartment for the first round of decluttering. Brian said hello to my sister and left, and my sister and I got to work. Suddenly, my sister yelled for me to come into her room. She said she found something, and there was a note of urgency in her voice that told me this was important. Before showing me what she found, she explained that there were some photos that had slipped out of a book she was packing up. The photos, she said, showed me in compromising positions. I mentally put on my suit of armor so nothing could get through, and I took a look. There was a Polaroid, likely taken with my own camera because I had been obsessed with that thing as a kid, and a few snapshots taken with a regular camera. I could not have been older than 3 in one of the photos; others were of me when I was slightly older. All of them were inappropriate. I was sick to my stomach and devastated. No matter how sure I had been that this had happened, these photos were evidence.

They were also validation, vindication even. I was right, and a sense of relief washed over me even as I was sickened by what I saw. The knowledge that this had happened to me had always been shadowed by doubt, a sort of second-guessing of myself and my memory that most victims of molestation experience. Because I had learned to live in a fantasy world where I had made up stories about my life, and because my mom had completely disregarded what I told her had happened, I could never fully trust myself. When I saw those photos, a part of me was like, "Right on. Never ever give up on your gut." It just showed me that, even in the most confusing and traumatic circumstances, your inner voice (or a higher power or your intuition – whatever you want to call it) will guide you and prevail. Now I am the only person I trust when it comes to me.

I stared at those photos voraciously, trying to get a handle on what I was looking at. All the years of confusion, doubt and fear were right there in a handful of pictures staring back at me. I cried for the little girl who lost her innocence so young. I cried that I was right all along. I cried that I ever questioned myself. My sister told me that she remembered finding the photos when we lived in New Jersey, but she couldn't recall where they had been exactly. She just instinctively knew when she saw them that they were important and she should take them for safekeeping. She was too young to know why. There's some intuition for you!

Of all the photos, one in which I was about 7 stood out most to me. It contrasted so sharply with the one where I was about 3, and you could still see my innocence, sweetness and vulnerability. I was adorable in that early picture: vibrant and not yet damaged. In the one where I was older, all the life had vanished from my face. The abuse had clearly taken its toll by that point, and if I had seen that girl at school or in the neighborhood, I probably would not have wanted to be friends with her either. Poor girl who had to endure so much pain and heartache and was only trying to survive by pushing away everything good in her life.

Obviously, these photos brought up a lot of memories for me. At that point, I began to tell my sister a little about what had happened to me. We had always had a deep love for each other, but we had never been close as children. (That would come later. Today, as adults, we are very close friends.) Flashbacks became my new norm. I would have nightmares, and Brian would wake me up to comfort me. Honestly, he was amazing as he shepherded me through the first clear phase of reliving this trauma.

Once I got over the shock and realized that I wasn't crazy, I decided to investigate further. It was 1998, and a good friend of mine worked for a private investigator at the time. The investigator researched Dave and discovered several disturbing things which convinced me that I had to take action. Some of these pertained to Dave's career as an attorney. It turned out his license had been suspended several times before he would eventually be disbarred in 1999. He had been privately reprimanded for gross neglect and failure to expedite litigation, among other things, in 1988. Then, 10 years later, he was suspended for three months for similar infractions, including a pattern of neglect, lack of diligence, failure to communicate, failure to promptly deliver funds to a client and failure to cooperate with the disciplinary authorities. In addition, 12 formal complaints had been filed against him at the district level. The complaints included a variety of allegations, including gross neglect (nine allegations), misrepresentation (two), failure to promptly deliver funds (two) and failure to turn over a file (one).

What was interesting was that Dave's disbarment would essentially stem from a call that he had made to a psychiatric emergency hotline in 1994. During that call, he allegedly told a hotline counselor that he was a child molester who lived in an apartment above a daycare center and that he had been molesting about eight or nine boys under the age of 2 for the past two years. He also claimed that he occasionally took care of the children at the daycare center for the owner, that he provided childcare for a living and that he would continue to molest young boys. The hotline counselor located his telephone number through a caller-identification system and immediately notified the police. A subsequent investigation by the Fort Lee police in New Jersey revealed that Dave did in fact live above a daycare center, but the center's director informed the police that it had solid security and that no one could gain admittance without authorization.

Why the police apparently took the daycare director's word for it is beyond me. As far as I know, there was no additional questioning of children or parents. Was the director just covering up to protect the daycare's business? Did Dave just not fit the profile of a molester for the police? It's almost like the system is set up to let things like that slip through the cracks. It seems obvious to me that, if a man confesses to being a molester, the police should assume it's true and search high and low for corroborating evidence rather than say, "Oh, the guy claims he was lying. I'll take his word for it." In my opinion, making any assertion that you've molested a child, even if it's later retracted, should raise a lot of red flags. Even if such a person were in fact lying (and Dave certainly wasn't, but let's just suppose this for the sake of argument), getting off on pretending to be a molester presents its own set of issues. Who knows what a person like that might be capable of? That's why, no matter if the claim itself is true or false, it seems like the police should have a legal and moral obligation to thoroughly investigate such people.

That same police investigation also revealed Dave had placed six calls to various agencies over the course of approximately six months between 1993 and 1994. Each time, he made similar confessions. The police learned that he had been investigated in 1989 as well, that time for a telephone call to a different hotline in which he told a social worker that he "babysat" and molested several children. When subsequently interviewed by the police for that call, Dave denied that he molested children even while admitting to having made the calls. No charges were pressed at that time.

In 1993, the Fort Lee police learned from an out-of-state police department that Dave had also made calls to a hotline in that state.

Apparently, he had called the hotline twice to confess to molesting 2- and 3-year-old children. When arrested by the Fort Lee police in 1994, Dave denied molesting any children. Instead, he claimed that he derived sexual gratification from calling help hotlines.

Dave was indicted in 1994 for two of these incidents (but not actual child molestation) and pleaded guilty to the second count, which charged him with the fourth-degree crime of false public alarm. He was sentenced to two years' probation under the conditions that he continue his treatment with his current therapist, that his therapist send reports to Dave's probation officer every two months, that he continue with the medication his psychiatrist prescribed and that he complete 100 hours of community service if he were accepted into a community-service program. Dave failed to report this conviction to the Office of Attorney Ethics, which, in light of Dave's indictment, conviction and other disciplinary measures, decided to disbar him.

This information, some of which was provided by the private-investigation company, some of which I later found myself, revealed just how much Dave's life had spiraled out of control. I guess the same darkness that destroyed my childhood haunted him his entire life. Something had to be done.

For the second time in my life, and with the support of Brian and my parents (by that time, my dad knew about the abuse), I went to meet with an assistant district attorney, and I brought the photos. Unfortunately, by the late 1990s, the statute of limitations had passed. While he couldn't be charged criminally, charges could be pressed that would enable the enforcement of Megan's Law, a federal law that requires the disclosure of information to the public regarding registered sex offenders. (Megan's Law was named after Megan Kanka, who was 6 years old when she was raped and killed by her neighbor in 1994.)

I was not looking to hurt or punish Dave. I was looking to stop a very sick man from hurting anyone else. While I had not yet arrived at the point where I had forgiven him (stay tuned), I knew his everyday life was miserable and no one would willingly choose to live the way he was living.

I began gathering evidence to support the photos and, as part of that process, I scheduled a lunch with Dave's ex-wife, whom I'd always loved and with whom I remain close to this day. While she could not answer all of my questions, she did give me some insight into her relationship with Dave and the dysfunctional person he was. I also spoke with other family members and people who knew him who would share their own experiences and insights. Soon, a picture began to emerge of a sexual deviant and predator. Dave was known to dress as a woman, engage in disturbingly violent role-play and solicit prostitutes even when he was in a relationship. And that was just the mainstream stuff. While I am not here to pass judgment on anyone else interested in those things, they and other behaviors made a lot of sense in light of Dave also being a child molester.

I continued on my quest to understand the mind of this man and to uncover any other information that would support my case. What I learned about his family of origin actually brought me to a place of understanding and forgiveness. There had always been whispers about the demons in my mom's side of the family. Those are not my stories to tell, but they did help me realize some monsters are born and others are created. As much as I hated Dave and what he had done to me, I began to realize that whatever had been done to him to make him into the person he became had to have been just as bad or worse. And without the resources or inner strength to deal with what had happened to him, it was no wonder he became a predator who repeated these devastating patterns. That was when I knew with absolute certainty that I had to do my best to stop the cycle.

One suggestion that the prosecuting attorney made was to try to record a call with Dave in which he would incriminate himself by admitting what he did. (In the state where the abuse had occurred, and where we were pressing charges, this was legal at the time.) I went to the police station a few times to make that call, but

Dave never answered. One night, in a moment of weakness when I was at home, I decided to call him again. I should not have done that, because I was not recording the call, and if he had admitted anything, it would not have been admissible in court. To my surprise, his girlfriend answered the phone. I had met her many times, and she was absolutely lovely but also subservient and passive. I said hello and then asked her, "Do you know what he did to me?"

She asked me why I was doing this, and I told her it was because he had abused me. She could choose to believe it, or she could close her eyes to it, but I told her she knew deep down that it was true and, furthermore, he probably didn't treat her right either. She answered, "He says he didn't do it." And then I heard her scream, "Ouch! Stop pinching me; that hurts." He was clearly trying to quiet her down. Soon, the line went dead. That was the end of any communication between me and either of them.

TIPS & TAKEAWAYS

Facing the Truth – Accepting the Truth

I knew all along what had happened to me, the abuse I had endured. Yet whenever I talked about it with others or with myself, I always hedged by saying that I couldn't be sure, or there was no evidence or, "I would never want to falsely accuse someone." All the while, I knew deep in my heart, deep in my soul, that this was real. It had happened.

Why did I continue to betray myself and the little girl I once was by wrapping my statements in doubt? I needed, unfortunately, hard evidence to believe myself. Once I found the evidence in the form of photos and other accusations against my abuser, there was no more hiding. It was time to face and accept the truth.

When life demands this of us, we have an opportunity to open our eyes and move forward.

This is how to begin:

1. **Admit there is a problem**: Until you get real with yourself and own what is going on, you won't be able to change your situation. That includes making it better.
2. **Look in the mirror**: Well, not literally, although you can do that too. But really look at the good, the bad and the ugly of who you are. Admit and accept what is. Then release what isn't serving you.
3. **Embrace the freedom of humility**: You have to humble yourself enough to face your true self, not the image or mask you wear each day. This can be daunting, but it can also be liberating. You have nothing to lose, except the stuff you want to change, by owning who you are to yourself.
4. **Get to know yourself**: Discover your strengths and weaknesses. The more in tune you are with yourself, the more you can face the truth and, ultimately, accept it.
5. **Don't let fear stand in your way**: Fear will only hold you back. When you seek and embrace the truth – about yourself or your situation – you only move forward. Seek the path you are meant to travel!

CHAPTER 17

Facing and accepting the reality of my past with Brian by my side strengthened our bond and made us stronger than ever. I would sob uncontrollably, and he would hold me. I would have night terrors, and he would console me. I would talk badly about myself, and he would remind me that I was beautiful and amazing and that he loved me.

On top of revisiting the trauma of my past, I still had to contend with my dad's erratic behavior. Brian was one of the only people close to my dad who was not intimidated by him, and he would defend me the same way I would defend my mom. I felt awful that he was put in that position yet, at the same time, I needed that so badly: a defender, an advocate, someone who saw the crazy and still had my back. My dad could be a monster of a different kind. In addition to the alcoholism, he suffered from obsessive-compulsive disorder (OCD) and had major impulsivity issues. Add to that a vision impairment that he developed in his 30s and that severely disabled him, and you can imagine how he would overcompensate for his perceived weakness.

The OCD took many forms. Sometimes my dad would move the cars around in the driveway of his and my mom's weekend house just to line them up more evenly. Sometimes he would transfer firewood from one pile to another, or alphabetize the pantry items.

Given all this, just think how he might react when someone left something out of order.

I remember one particular incident when I left the light on in the basement of my parents' weekend house. When my dad found out, he lost it on me! He gave me a verbal beating, calling me stupid, lazy and spoiled, even though the light hadn't been left on longer than a day. It was the sort of overreaction I had grown up with, and I took it, but Brian was not having it. With a few sharp words, he put an end to it, and my dad never lost it like that on me again. My fiancé was saving me in some very important ways from a life I previously had no control over. He helped me to learn how to love myself, and he was offering me an out.

While my relationship with Brian had its ups and downs, it was solid. And life was pretty amazing! We were living in Manhattan in the late '90s. I was a special-education teacher with a candy company on the side (I was always of an entrepreneurial mind); Brian was working on Wall Street. This was the height of the tech boom, and the traders were living large. We would go out to dinner with his friends at the trendiest restaurants, and the guys would play credit-card roulette to decide who would pick up the check. These outings could easily cost $500 or more. The credit cards would go into a hat or a bowl. The waitress would remove the credit cards one by one, and you definitely wanted to hear your name because the last credit card would be the one charged.

It was crazy. These were young guys in their mid- to late 20s, and they were living the good life, many of them making seven figures. We would get box seats at sporting events with dinners that were as good as those at some of the restaurants we frequented. We vacationed at the top spots, had front-row seats at boxing matches, reserved the best seats at concerts – you name it, we experienced it. Even though we weren't married yet, it was like Brian and I had joined this exclusive club. I was finally being accepted and viewed as normal. I finally had all the right labels. The questions were always the same: What do you do? Where do you live? Have you been to this restaurant or vacation destination? And on and on. Forget about keeping up with the Joneses. I was determined to *be* the Joneses!

At the time, that filled me up. I thought that was what life was all about. What an ego I was trying to fill!

The same voice that had always guided me was still there, only this time I was ignoring it. I knew it was there, but I couldn't get in touch with it enough to trust it. There was definitely a small part of me that was yearning for more, but I was so immersed in that life, and it felt so much better than my previous life, that I probably couldn't have found a crack to escape from even if I had wanted to. Instead, I used all these masks, labels and titles to distract myself and numb the pain that was still there.

The truth was I still felt horrible, and getting out of my parents' place, meeting my fiancé and having the best of everything was never going to provide the peace and happiness I so desperately sought. Unbeknown to me at the time, the only thing that was going to do that was going inward.

For the time being, however, I was focused on everything around me, especially my wedding. Brian was a romantic who didn't shy away from grand gestures. Once, during a Yankees game, he buried a beautiful ring in a bag of popcorn, just because. And his proposal was just as much of a surprise. We had talked about marriage, but at 22, I didn't think it was happening anytime soon. Little did I know that he'd already asked my parents' permission and spoken to my sister. So one evening, when we were in our apartment together, he just asked. He presented me with an exceptionally beautiful ring, and I accepted. We went downstairs to share the good news with my sister (she lived in the same building) and then to visit my parents before going out with friends to celebrate. It was a perfect proposal – warm, intimate and loving.

The wedding itself, meanwhile, took a different direction. Everything, from our engagement to our reception, was designed to impress. We had multiple engagement parties for family, for friends, for out-of-towners – you name it, we found a way to turn it into a celebration. And wow, our wedding was something that I will never forget. But when you get so immersed in the planning of something (in this case, our wedding celebrations), you can sometimes lose sight of what is in front of you (in this case, our actual relationship). We were so focused on the day-to-day stuff – work, socializing and wedding planning – that we were on autopilot. We weren't taking time to enjoy each moment, let alone step back and assess the situation. So, while we were busy checking off all the boxes for planning our wedding and earning the approval of those around us, we were forgetting to stay focused on one major box: OUR RELATIONSHIP! If I could offer one piece of advice, it would be to remind everyone that the fairy tale can exist but not unless you nurture the actual relationship. That is the foundation upon which all else will be built.

There were many amazing things that came out of my wedding-planning experience, not least of which was the time I spent with my mom. She did everything with me, and while she was caught up in the one piece of it that no longer resonates with me (how everything appeared), that doesn't matter. The time we had together was invaluable, especially the lunches and cab rides between appointments where, fresh off the high of having found the perfect dress or venue, we could just talk. She shared so many of her thoughts on marriage and my life during those times. The whole process gave me memories that I still take pleasure in revisiting.

I have to say that, despite the outcome of our marriage, our wedding was spectacular! It was lavish, but it was also elegant and sophisticated. Actually, the whole weekend was tremendous! We spent Thursday night at Bowlmor Lanes with the out-of-town guests and the wedding party, followed by the rehearsal dinner on Friday night at F.illi Ponte. After the rehearsal dinner, we went for drinks at Mickey Mantle's, which is just steps away from The Plaza, where we got married. Our wedding was on Saturday, and we had his-and-her suites at the hotel so that the guys could have wings and watch football before the ceremony while my bridal party and I had our hair and makeup done.

The wedding itself was magical with no expense spared. *Modern Bride* magazine featured the whole event. During cocktail hour, guests mingled over caviar, lobster and Dom Pérignon, while intricately carved ice sculptures formed an elegant backdrop. Our florist was a celebrity himself and for good reason. He displayed flowers in giant picture frames along the balcony seats for an almost three-dimensional effect. We had two bands and the food ranged from sushi and caviar to lobster and lamb. A Sunday brunch followed at my parents' place before the big send-off. People still talk with me about how my wedding was one of the best they've ever attended. Yes, it was over the top, but what really made it stand out was how, despite having almost 300 people in attendance, the room was filled with warmth and love. It felt intimate. Exactly the emotions Brian and I wanted to evoke!

While I look back on it with fondness and gratitude, I also know that I would never have a celebration like that again for myself. (Even if I had a partner who wanted that, although it's unlikely I'd be with someone who would.) There is nothing wrong with any of it, of course, but that no longer represents any part of who I am. Back then, the opulence validated my ego, but at the end of the day, I was an empty vessel. Today, I am no longer that person. That type of attention does not fuel or support me. While I am the first to admit that I enjoy nice things, those things do not define me as they once did. Now, my perfect night includes a nice, homemade dinner; getting some work done; hanging with my kids and significant other (when I have one); and watching Netflix by my fire pit. The life I currently live is not as flashy, but it makes me so much happier because it is aligned with my authentic self.

Soon after the wedding, as Brian and I settled into what was supposed to be marital bliss, we developed some habits that were not healthy for us as individuals and especially not as a couple. Brian would keep busy with work or go out at night while I stayed home, for example. We also criticized each other, even as we loved and supported each other. These habits were creating distance between us, but neither of us could see what was happening at the time. And if we got glimpses of it, we swept it under the rug. Neither of us had the necessary communication skills to support the kind of healthy conversations we needed. Looking back now, I realize that I had picked up some of my mom's ambivalence. The relationship continued at that level. We enjoyed our two dogs and figuring out life together, seeing friends and family, celebrating various occasions and just being married despite the increasing distance and conflict. If we were to follow the societal norms, which we were, then the next logical step would be to have children. And since that definitely matched up with my desires, it was a no-brainer.

TIPS & TAKEAWAYS

Embracing Happiness

The time around my marriage was one of the first when I experienced some kind of real happiness. I had started healing old wounds with the support of my wonderful partner and, at the time, that made me feel whole and complete. We also had some amazing experiences together that allowed me to grow and develop the confidence that I longed for. I finally felt safe and protected, which permitted me to stop the sabotage and embrace the good things that were happening in my life.

You don't need to get married or find love, however, to find happiness. Sometimes, it's as easy as being open to it.

1. **Experience gratitude**: It's pretty simple. Gratitude is everything! When you focus on what you are grateful for, on what good things are already in your life, you're just

naturally going to experience more happiness and joy. It also invites more good things into your life!

2. **Live in the moment**: All there is, all you have, is this very moment. Rather than worrying about the future (which is largely out of your control) or ruminating over the past (which you can't change), you can control how you feel in the present. Choose happiness.

3. **Smile**: Studies have shown that smiling releases endorphins (natural painkillers) and serotonin, a chemical in our bodies that plays a key role in mood, sleep, digestion and other key functions. Together, they make us feel good from head to toe. Enough said!

4. **Be open**: Maybe things aren't going as planned. Maybe someone, or all of society, thinks you should be doing things differently. But if you take that noise out of the equation and keep an open mind, you might find some good stuff in your life that can set you on a path to happiness.

5. **Forgive**: One of the biggest misconceptions around forgiveness is that it lets the other person off the hook. In reality, it frees you from the negative energy that binds you to the offending party. When you hold on to anger, sadness, hurt, contempt or dissatisfaction – whether toward yourself or another person – then you allow the grievance to continue to hurt you. This is why it is so important to forgive. You do it not because someone else deserves it but because *you* deserve peace.

CHAPTER 18

I knew right away when I was pregnant. I could feel it. The same intuition that I'd always had was rearing its head again.

And this time it was super exciting! I could not believe this day had finally come. I had always had so much love to give, and I wanted more than anything to share that with my children.

The day I took the at-home test and found out I was pregnant, Brian was laid up with a back injury and was in too much pain to celebrate. I was okay with that because I was happy and excited enough for the both of us (and then some)! A few weeks later, we went to the doctor to confirm what the stick had shown us, and wow, were we in for a surprise. Looking at the screen, the doctor said, "I see a heartbeat!" So it was true, I was pregnant...we were pregnant! Then the doctor said, "Uh oh." Brian and I looked at each other, and one of us asked, "Is everything okay?" The doctor quickly recovered and replied, "I see a second heartbeat!" What?! We were having twins! For the first time in my life, I experienced pure joy. I didn't question it, and there weren't any negative feelings attached to it. It was just pure joy! I walked out of the doctor's office floating – this couldn't have been better news. I think Brian walked out just as excited but perhaps slightly more shocked!

It was a joyful time for both of us as we prepared for the birth of our boys, sharing the news with everyone and just getting emotionally and psychologically prepared for this new chapter in our lives. It became a full-time job! In our circle, there were unspoken expectations about where you would shop for maternity clothing, where you would buy baby clothes and gear, which classes you would sign up for and so on. It was as though everything had to be just so or something would fall apart. I remember running into people, and the checklist was always the same. Did you go to this boutique? Will you have a baby nurse? Will you breastfeed or use formula? Which pediatrician are you going to? The list went on and on…and the judgment was loud and clear! I was the first in our circle to get pregnant, but I found myself doing the same thing to other women as they announced their pregnancies. Why did it even matter? Why were we bonding over inconsequential stuff like that? But at the time, I didn't question it. I was on cloud nine!

Work was also going well for me. Before I got married, I earned my master's in education at Columbia University, where I discovered my passion for working with children. After my wedding, I worked in special education at an elementary school. The schedule was perfect, because teaching gave me a couple of hours each afternoon to work on my other business: a candy company called The Sweet Life that I'd launched with a friend from graduate school. We catered to large corporations and customized personal gifts, and the orders were pouring in! I loved both careers: The candy company scratched my itch for entrepreneurship while teaching fulfilled my purpose of taking care of others and helping children.

As we settled into our new life and the noise and excitement started to fade, I often wondered if Brian and I were really happy, if I were happy, or if we were just fulfilling societal expectations. Basically, I wondered if we were living from an authentic place or if we were simply following conditioned behaviors. I wasn't sure why this was coming up for me. We both had solid jobs, and Brian was a high earner; we had great friends and family surrounding us; we lived in an incredible duplex apartment on Central Park West; and we had two beautiful babies on the way. Why was I still empty? What was wrong with me?

We decided to start couples therapy. Even though he never said it, I always got the feeling that Brian blamed our problems on my "stuff." He wanted to support me and partner with me in working on the relationship, but I had been working through my stuff. Could it be that it was time to look at *his* stuff? Or, more importantly, was it time to look at our stuff as a couple? What I was realizing was that I wasn't the same person I was when we got married a year or two earlier, and I definitely wasn't the same person I was when we met. We were both growing as people, and I was starting to wonder if we were growing apart.

Brian was a drinker, but by the time I reached my early 20s, I was over it. He was also super social. Everyone loved him – you know that guy, the life of the party. I, on the other hand, preferred staying in. So he would go out after work and meet up with friends or clients – his job entailed a lot of entertaining – while I would stay home. Many nights, I would be asleep by the time he got home. I had no problem with this, because I was very happy at home by myself. I don't think he minded either, because he was out enjoying himself. It was a setup that also allowed us to avoid intimacy, which we both seemed to be fine with, at least on an unconscious level. There were some awesome times, yes. But looking back, I can see that the distance began even earlier than I thought.

All marriages have ups and downs. The question becomes, Do you love this person enough to go through the ups and downs together and come out the other side as a couple? We started therapy together early on not to save our marriage but to support it, to help it grow and develop. We knew problems would arise, and we wanted to develop the necessary skills to overcome them as a couple and in the healthiest way possible. But when we went to therapy together, somehow it always came back to my history. Not just the abuse but also my dad and the way my family operated in general. Truth be told, Brian came from just as much dysfunction – it was simply a different kind. While I didn't see it then, he was as much a contributor to the stress in our relationship as I was. I mean, we were just kids trying to figure it out. From that perspective, and despite the challenges, I think we did a pretty amazing job.

At about 26 weeks into my pregnancy, I started early labor. This is not too unusual when you are having twins, so I wasn't overly alarmed. We went to the hospital, and I was put on bed rest. As anyone who knows me can tell you, that is one of the absolute worst things I could have to do. I need to have the freedom to move around! But for those two babies, I would do anything. Because I was not allowed to walk upstairs, duplex living presented some challenges. Every morning, I would have to go into the hallway and take the elevator down one floor so I could spend the day in the main living area. Then, every evening, I would have to do the reverse so I could return to the bedroom. For weeks, I laid about the apartment, physically stagnant and uncomfortable. So when my doctor told me a few weeks before my due date that I could go off bed rest, I was elated. (At that point, it would be safe to go into labor at any time.)

The first day I was off bed rest was September 11, 2001. I could barely walk, I was so far along in my pregnancy, so I took a cab to Tower Records on West 67th Street. I was going to pick up some soothing CDs for the babies. In the cab, the radio was on and then, all of a sudden, it went silent. I checked my Motorola flip phone only to see that I had lost cell service. I paid the cabdriver and, confused, I walked into Tower Records a little less excited than I had been when I left the house. When I entered the store, I knew something was amiss but I couldn't figure out what. I decided to skip the purchase and go home. Maybe bed rest wasn't so bad after all! I got in the cab, and there was still no cell service but the radio was working. Suddenly I heard, "A plane went through the Twin Towers." I asked the driver to turn up the radio, and I listened until I got home. Brian was supposed to be at a meeting at the Twin Towers! The phone wasn't working, I was 10 days away from having two babies and I was worried. I got to the landline and called Brian at work and on his cell, but there was no answer.

My mom, sister and aunt made their way to my place. Though Brian's phone wasn't working, somehow all our friends' phones worked, and everyone was calling to see if I had heard from him. We were glued to the television for what seemed like hours. Then it came. The phone rang with an unfamiliar number. I answered hesitantly, afraid of what I might hear, but it was him. He was okay. Thank goodness, he was okay. His plans had changed that morning, and he was across the bridge in Jersey City when the World Trade Center collapsed. He would have to walk home, but he was alive. He said he didn't have long – it was a pay phone and there was a long line – but what he had experienced was horrible. He'd seen people jumping out of windows, people covered in ash – it was pure chaos. I told him I was so happy to hear his voice and to hurry home. My family waited to see and hug him before leaving to let us catch up on everything that had happened. It was awful. I was so sorry he'd had to see what he had seen, but I was also grateful that he was one of the lucky ones. Wall Street was our community – those were our people – and so many of our friends lost loved ones that day.

That night, we got in the car and drove around the city. I had never seen New York that way, and it was surreal. People were wandering aimlessly around, and we, like many others, offered them rides home. On what day in New York City would you ever consider picking up strangers and driving them home? Only on that day. There was no transportation – the buses and subways were shut down and no cabs were in sight. We knew how long my husband had had to walk, and we wanted to help others if we could. The following day, we made sandwiches for the first responders and everyone else who was pitching in. We lived in a bit of a haze during that time. I just remember wondering over and over again how such a tragedy could happen when two miracles were just days away from being born. It did not make sense to me. It did not make sense to anyone, because it was a senseless tragedy that came from hate, ignorance and anger.

On September 21, those two miracles entered the world. Michael and Alexander. They were everything I was expecting and more.

How was I the luckiest person alive?! Had things gone differently, my boys might have been like so many other children impacted by 9/11 and never known their dad. Instead, I was beyond fortunate to have all three of them. And my good luck wasn't lost on me. Was this the reward for everything I'd endured? If so, I would go through that trauma over and over again. I was in love.

Our little world revolved around those two baby boys. They were showered with love and attention by everyone who came into contact with them. Not just because they were the first grandchildren, and in fact the first babies, to join our family in a very long time but also because, when there is such an enormous tragedy, people need good things to grab on to. What's better than a newborn baby? Two newborn babies!

TIPS & TAKEAWAYS

Finding Light in the Darkness

"There is mud, and there is the lotus that grows out of the mud. We need the mud in order to make the lotus." – *Thich Nhat Hanh*

Like those of so many others, my life has been a struggle between darkness and light. I have always sought the light, but much of my life, especially the early years, was spent in the darkness. Sometimes moments of light pierced through, like when Rusty appeared in my life or when we moved to the city and I could stop the cycle of abuse and create a new life for myself. Those glimmers kept me going. Although I couldn't articulate it at the time, I leaned toward the light. I knew that was not just *where* I wanted to be but *what* I wanted to be. Before I could become that beam radiating throughout, however, I first had to climb out of the darkness.

Here is how I did so:

1. **Appreciate the dark**: Your darkest hours are merely a setup for your greatest days to come.

2. **Never give up on yourself**: Sometimes it can seem like the results you want will never arrive. This is part of the process. If you practice self-love with patience and consistency, positive change will follow.

3. **Have courage**: Regardless of what the darkness may be for you, be courageous in noticing it, fighting through it, not letting it consume you and coming out the other side.

4. **Be purposeful about what you give your energy to**: Not everything needs your attention or response. When you can't remove yourself from toxic relationships or situations, create as much distance as possible between you and them. This can look many different ways, from not reacting to a trigger to refusing to concentrate your thoughts on people or situations that don't deserve your awareness.

5. **Get support from family, friends and loved ones**: A critical component of moving from darkness to light is surrounding yourself with people who are uplifting, who have your best interests at heart and who want to see you thrive.

6. **Be aware of your resistance to change**: Many people have a fear of change or of the unknown, and they unconsciously reside in a state of resistance. This is one way that people trap themselves in the darkness they so badly want to leave behind. The first step to any change is to become more aware of your thoughts, of how your body feels and of what your triggers are.

7. **Be fearless about removing negativity from your life**: Have the confidence to say, "I deserve better than that," and then make the necessary changes that will lead to a life full of light.

CHAPTER 19

I slid into motherhood with ease and comfort. I had always been good with babies and kids, and I think that had to do with the empathy I developed as a result of my experiences. Motherhood was my calling, and I had finally found my purpose. Taking care of those two little guys day and night was pretty much perfection, and the issues between me and their dad seemed to fall by the wayside. There were so many milestones to celebrate over the next two and a half years that it was easy to put the blinders on for any conflict, distance or frustration.

Just to clarify: In case you think, *Of course there were issues! Every relationship goes through ups and downs, and part of getting through the downs is working through them together and independently*, this was different; the issues were different.

Instead of facing our situation, though, we distracted ourselves with first birthdays, promotions, family celebrations and the tragic passing of my father-in-law. There was also the matter of selling our apartment and leaving the only place I ever really called home: New York City. With two babies and a third on the way, it was time to relocate to the family-friendly suburbs. And the move came just in time. We closed on our new home in November 2003, had some work done to the house and then moved in in March 2004. I gave birth to my perfect little girl, Jessica, that April.

At 7 pounds, 4 ounces, she was the most positive significant event in my life other than the birth of my boys. She had a fierce and strong personality, and you could tell she was going to be a fighter just like her mom. (And a fighter she is!) She was a dream come true! While I definitely wanted more children, I knew our beautiful little girl completed our family. I was on top of the world!

True to form, the day I got home from the hospital, I was back at the grocery store stocking up for the boys and for family and friends who were sure to visit our third miracle. I never took a break, and that was not necessarily a good thing. Back then, I was an overachiever who derived validation from getting it all done at a high level. That was definitely a characteristic that raised the question, *Why?* What was I chasing? While I still tend to take a lot on and don't love to ask for help, I no longer have to be the best at everything, and I don't mind saying, "No" or "I can't."

Doing it all at a very high level can be empowering and fulfilling in many ways, but it can also leave you exhausted and create resentment within a partnership. Had I known then what I know now, I would have asked for help when I wanted or needed it – and even when I didn't – instead of taking it all on. I used to get annoyed and a little passive aggressive when I would do it all and Brian wouldn't offer to pitch in or even get up. He probably just assumed that I was fine doing it all. How could he know what I wanted if I didn't tell him?

Being a mother to three children under 3 was daunting but exciting. Juggling that and my thriving entrepreneurial career, as well as being a wife in the way that I wanted to be, required a lot of creativity, and I rose to the occasion. Our new home, however, only added to the pressure. I had to face a lot of fears when I agreed to move out of the city. While I'd had my driver's license since I was 17 years old and would often drive to visit friends and family out of the city, I was nervous about *having* to drive, about driving all the time, about driving in snow, about finding my way around and about all the other things that go hand-in-hand with driving. I was also nervous not to have a doorman to protect me. People often think living in the city is dangerous, and I get that. But from my perspective, the city offered me a safe building with a doorman as the gatekeeper. The suburbs, on the other hand, laid out the welcome mat to anyone who wanted to come in, including Dave. Yes, I had an alarm system, and yes, I realize some of these thoughts were unrealistic. But they were real for me at the time. I had come a long way from the scared little girl I had been, but relocating raised issues that revealed I hadn't come as far as I thought I had. While I wasn't happy about it, I guess the reminder was necessary if I wanted to keep evolving into the best version of myself possible. It was once again time to face my demons.

Shortly after I gave birth to Jessica, the flashbacks returned and they were getting worse. My daughter was just a baby, but her very presence was bringing up images for me that I couldn't avoid. After all, I was just a few years older than Jessica when I was first abused. I realized that if I didn't take care of this as soon as possible, I would project my issues onto her and my boys, and I absolutely did not want to do that to any of them. When I decided to become a parent, I took the responsibility very seriously, and part of being the best parent I could be meant healing myself.

The moment had come for me to get into therapy again. But this time it was purely my own choice. Yet, even with that momentum, it wasn't smooth sailing. After several tries with different therapists, I began to feel defeated. I just could not find the right fit, which was frustrating because I was actually ready this time. I was starting to wonder if it were me. Was I being too selective, or was I just scared of the work ahead?

I knew I had to show up for this, and that meant finding the right therapist. That had to become my number-one priority. I was determined to break the cycle and start a new paradigm for our family. I took on the search for a therapist as if it were a full-time job. Eventually, I was referred to an expert in psychoanalytic psychotherapy who has authored many books on the subject. I knew it was a long shot, but I emailed her to see if she could recommend someone based on my experience and location. She responded within 24 hours and recommended a man who was literally a seven-minute walk from my home! This is the beauty of intention and manifestation.

I met with him, and although the experience of adult psychoanalysis was intimidating and uncomfortable, I knew it would take something drastic to make a dent in my healing. And it helped. I spent many painful, challenging and exciting years untangling the mess I grew up in. Actually, it is 15 years later, and while I am at a completely different level than I was when I started, I am still unraveling it all and probably will be for the rest of my life. It was so complicated, and each topic had so much ground to cover, but I was committed and ready to begin.

With growth comes change, and, boy, did I change. I grew as a mother, a woman, a wife and a friend. I grew as a spiritual being. And I grew out of the issues that had haunted and defined me for most of my life. Gradually, I morphed into the person who had been hidden for most of my life, and I was starting to like – no, I was starting to love – who I was.

With this personal growth came another change. Shortly after my daughter was born, I realized I no longer wanted to teach or run my candy company. I wanted a career with a more flexible schedule, and I wanted to do something that did not involve kids. For me, working with children required every ounce of my energy and focus. I needed to devote that to my own children if I were going to fulfill the commitment I made to them and to myself when I decided to become a parent. So I brainstormed lots of options, and the one that made the most sense was real estate. Years earlier, back in New York, Brian had suggested real estate to me as a career option. He told me he thought I would kill it, but I wasn't open to it then. In truth, I did not have enough confidence in myself to even consider it. At this point, however, it seemed much more viable and interesting. I had always thrived at sales and had been in and out of it professionally since I was 15 years old. I also enjoyed making my own money, and I knew that if I were able to sell real estate at a high level, it could be very lucrative. So, a close friend and I went to real estate school and obtained our licenses. Honestly, I never thought I would go back to school after finishing my master's degree. But if I have a goal, I do what I need to do to accomplish it. So I got my license, and my friend and I decided to partner up and start a real estate business together. The beauty of this partnership was our compatibility. We were great friends, our spouses were close and our kids were the same ages. So she and I could watch each other's children when handling clients if our spouses were unavailable. It was a great situation, and our first year proved it.

During this time, I was also going deep with my therapy. I mean, I was in it. So much so that much of the work would happen in between the appointments rather than during the sessions. I spent a lot of my downtime processing everything that was coming up for me. This wasn't just the abuse and my family dynamics and who I was as a person. It was also my relationship with my husband and my dissatisfaction with it. At this point, our daughter was around 4 years old and our boys were 6. I had spent a lot of time unpacking the trauma of my childhood, and I was now focusing on how to improve my relationship with my spouse.

I don't think Brian or I had any idea about what we signed up for when we decided that therapy would be the next best step, both for us individually and for us as a couple. I don't think we realized that therapy doesn't just address an isolated issue. Instead, when you deal with the presenting issue, the work naturally spreads into all other areas of life. I was changing and growing at a rapid rate. I no longer recognized myself, and while I was loving the transformation, I was not the person Brian married. This was confusing and unfamiliar to both of us. On one hand, I was excelling at work and gaining confidence. On the other, I needed to be out of the house more often to attend to my clients. I also had new wants and needs – and I wasn't shy about standing up for them.

While Brian had initially been supportive of my new career, neither of us could've predicted what it was going to mean for our relationship or our life. Brian didn't like it. Or what I should probably say is that he was fine with it until it impacted him. For example, if a presentation ran late, he would have to take care of the kids or prepare the meals, duties that ordinarily fell to me with him filling in now and then. Whenever circumstances required us to switch these roles, he seemed irritated and frustrated with me. I was equally frustrated and confused because I felt like there were mixed messages. *Go get your real estate license! You are going to kill it, and I support you! Wait – why do I have to make dinner? Who's going to put the kids to bed?* He grew angry and passive-aggressive when my work required him to step up in ways he wasn't used to and probably didn't want to do. Once again, just as with my parents, the message was clear: Follow your path as long as it's within the box that I have set forth and approve of.

At the time, I could not make sense of it, but now I understand what he was experiencing. He was watching me transform and succeed and garner a great deal of attention for the success. This was different from what we had both been accustomed to. It caused even more space and distance between us. That, combined with our lives growing in different directions, set us on a course for destruction. It wasn't a question of whether the ball would drop. It was a question of when.

TIPS & TAKEAWAYS

Being Okay With Not Having It All Figured Out

As you can see, life has never been a straight line for me. And what fun would that be anyway? When I was younger, I spent a good deal of time trying to follow what was expected of me, but I was always pulled back to following my heart. Once I accepted that, I was able to understand that not only is my quirky, roundabout path okay, but it is also a normal (in its own way) part of life. You don't have to have it all together! The whole point of living a full life is embracing the ups, the downs and the in-betweens.

Your life is your own. Live it your way!

1. **Go easy on yourself**: Despite what society would have you believe, it's actually impossible to have everything and every moment in your life be absolutely perfect. Your life can be messy and still get you where you want to go.
2. **Be okay with needing help**: Needing help does not mean you are weak. It actually demonstrates an immense amount of wisdom and strength. So go ahead and ask for it!
3. **Let go of expectations**: When you have a picture in your head of how things should be in your life, when you are so focused on not only where you want to go but what the path should be to get there, you set yourself up for disappointment. Life very rarely unfolds the way we plan. Let go, do the work and let your path unfold, even if unfolding doesn't happen as neatly as you'd like.
4. **Don't compare yourself to others**: You don't know what anyone else is going through. No matter what they look like on social media, no matter what masks they wear, no matter how big the house or fancy the car or perfect the relationship, I can promise you everyone is struggling in their own way. You're not behind or ahead but on your own path.

CHAPTER 20

By 2008 the ball had dropped. Brian and I decided to split up. After all the work – the marriage counseling, the communication, the trying to rekindle our romance – we reluctantly came to the conclusion that our marriage wasn't salvageable. And it was devastating. It felt like we went from being in love to falling out of love in the space of a moment. I did not know how things had changed so quickly.

They hadn't changed overnight. The signs were happening along the way; we just weren't seeing them. If we did see them, we weren't addressing them. By the time we did, it was over. I am the type of person that, once I realize something, it is hard to un-see it.

The pain of facing the perceived failure of our roles as a husband and wife, as a mom and dad, plus the hurt we were causing each other and could cause our children, was brutal. It felt like everything was crashing down on me at once.

What ensued was a storm of emotions. For me, the most difficult part was letting go of what I had built, of what we had built. We had worked hard to achieve a beautiful life with the nice house, the charming neighborhood, the three kids and two dogs and the prestigious job for him. When we had to face its dissolution, wow, it hurt. We had accomplished all that we had been told we needed to in order to have the life that we were taught to want – the life we thought we wanted. But what we were taught wasn't necessarily the truth, at least not for us.

Life has tons of twists and turns, and it's easy to sit in judgment of others and their situations until you are faced with something similar. I used to parade around on my high horse saying I would never get a divorce. That I would figure out a way to make it work. I was so self-righteous! So in my pain arrived a very meaningful lesson. I try very hard not to judge now, just as I try not to declare what I would or wouldn't do in certain situations. I don't have all the answers. Instead, all I try to do now is flow.

I knew Brian was hurting too. For 11 years, we had collaborated in love and in conflict and had so many amazing, life-changing experiences. The truth was we were young when we met. I had barely met myself at that point. Looking at it from the other side, I have no regrets about marrying Brian. What he gave me was tremendous – a love that I needed, three amazing children who have given my life a purpose I can't even put into words, friendship and experiences that allowed me to evolve into the person I am today.

To break it apart was depressing, sobering and surreal. We worried for ourselves, for each other and, perhaps most of all, for our children. The world of single-parenting was a mystery to us, and I found it scary and overwhelming. It was daunting enough to face the fact that the life we had built, the life I had believed was my future, was over. That we had three young kids who needed us to show up as our best selves and to be an anchor for them as they experienced and processed their emotions was a lot to ask of anyone. It was in that moment that I decided that, no matter what the situation was with Brian, no matter what my future life held, my kids were going to come first. They were always going to be my number-one priority. I had to approach the process mindfully and with them at the forefront of every decision. Don't get me wrong: That didn't mean that everything was perfect or that I didn't make mistakes along the way, because I did (lots of them) and it definitely wasn't perfect. However, when I reaffirmed the conscious decision I had made the first time I found out I was pregnant – to always put them first – I believe that allowed them to go through the divorce process as kindly and gently as possible.

It was not easy for any of us, and we each handled it in our own way, from retreating from the world (me) to socializing with everyone and finding as many fun distractions for the kids as possible (Brian). We didn't have any examples for how to go about this, so we were trailblazers whether we wanted to be or not! Other families with young kids weren't getting divorced yet, despite the fact there were many who were not only unhappy but downright miserable. They were intent on looking happy, though, on being the picture-perfect family. Never mind that behind each picture-perfect image there were usually a lot of secrets. Because of my real estate career, I pretty much knew everyone in town and, for some reason, people would confide in me about how unhappy they truly were. I guess I was always coaching, even when I didn't realize it! There was only one other family going through a divorce with a child in my boys' grade, and it was rumored to be nasty with the police being called to their home and the parents talking poorly about each other publicly. I did not want that for us.

I knew I could not control what Brian did, but I could control my own actions. I was purposeful and mindful and conscious, and I can confidently say that I tried my very best. I tried to be there for Brian, although it was tricky to do so without sending mixed messages to both him and the kids. Although I worked during our marriage, I primarily held the role of the traditional wife and mother, and I loved and embraced that. You see, despite cultivating a successful career and despite being fully capable of supporting myself mentally, physically and emotionally, I am a traditionalist when it comes to relationships. Call me old-fashioned, but I actually derive pleasure from taking care of my man in ways that women did back in the day. I am all for equality and believe that men and women deserve equal rights and equal pay. Part of that inherent equality, though, is being able to freely choose your roles. Some women prefer to leave domestic duties to their husbands or split them evenly with their partners. For me, I enjoy taking care of my partner, whether it's cooking a nice meal for him or attending to the details that make his life easier.

For Brian, this was also what he was accustomed to. I had taken care of him in some very important ways for many years, and I did not want to take that away from him all at once. So I continued to make meals for him and drop them off at his place when he had the kids and even when he didn't. I represented him as his Realtor when he rented his new place. For a while, I would even make his appointments, take care of insurance claims and handle various household responsibilities. He was struggling, and the more I could help, the better he would be for himself, for our kids and for me. Now, if you ask him, he may not recall it the same way, but I know what was in my heart. If he was not able to receive, I couldn't control that. I had to do my best by him and then, after a certain point, let go. My kids and I needed me more.

TIPS & TAKEAWAYS

Making the Tougher Decision

In my life I have had to make many difficult choices. There was a time when I would take the easy way out, and while that felt better in the moment, the feeling never lasted. When I started having harder conversations with both myself and others, and when I subsequently started choosing the more difficult option, it rarely felt good in the moment, but the effects were always more positive and enduring. So it came down to the ultimate choice of sorts: Did I want an easy fix that was temporary, or did I want to take the more difficult path and reap the long-term benefits?

I soon became an enthusiastic believer in the advantages of choosing the more difficult path. In challenging myself, I came out the other side to something better than I could have imagined. More importantly, I came out the other side to a better me, a better version of myself, each and every time. Make no mistake, there is nothing easy about this. Some situations may be easier than others, but in general, none is easy.

When faced with a difficult decision, it is tempting to rationalize taking the path of least resistance. You really have to want better for yourself and those you love to face your options dispassionately, evaluate them rationally and commit to the right choice even when it's the hard one. It can be hard to be confident about that choice. This is what I did over and over again when I told my parents about the abuse, when I faced my abuser, when I switched schools, when I decided to leave the illusion of the white-picket-fence life and get a divorce, when I changed careers intentionally and every time I opted to let go of what no longer served me.

The process begins with these simple steps:

1. **Take time to reflect**: Pay attention to what comes up for you. When you notice a pattern, when there's something gnawing at you, it is not just a passing thought. You need to listen.

2. **Notice your body's reaction**: Our bodies speak to us all day long. If something is not right in your life, there is a correlating physical component (like nausea, anxiety or shortness of breath) just as there is a correlating physical component when something is right (lightness, euphoria, clarity). Start paying attention to the information your body is providing you.

3. **Write a pros and cons list**: Creating a list around the positives and negatives of a decision allows you the clarity to know your options, learn your non-negotiables and evaluate your decision accordingly.

4. **Clear your mind**: It's okay to focus on the decision at hand, but make sure you are doing it productively and not getting caught up in the what-ifs.

5. **Think about both scenarios**: Visualize your life in both scenarios — staying the same or making the change — and you'll see that one resonates more with you, even if only slightly. Sometimes we know what the right decision is, but we struggle with the process of change and the stuff that goes along with it.

6. **Think in terms of years, not days**: Think about the long-term outcome, not the short-term pain.

CHAPTER 21

I remember the day we told our children. Michael and Alexander were 7 years old; Jessica was only 5. We were gathered around the kitchen table and, despite the strife and mixed emotions we felt toward each other, Brian and I presented a united front. I am proud of us for that. We supported each other in the best of ways during that painful and difficult conversation. It was an example of what we were capable of.

Clearly, the tension was high in the house by that point, and while the kids weren't outwardly demonstrating any evidence of knowing, they had to be aware on some level that something was going on. The energy simply felt different in the home. No matter how good you think you are at hiding things from your children, kids are intuitive beings by nature. Even if they can't pinpoint exactly what is happening, they are absolutely feeling it in some way.

Brian and I were determined to be honest with the kids without being all doom and gloom. We wanted to convey that, despite what we were going through as a family, and no matter what ups or downs might come out of it, Brian and I would always be there for them. We wanted them to see this as a new adventure that we would experience together – even if "together" looked a little different moving forward. We invited them to ask questions. Some we had the answers to, and some we didn't. When we didn't have the answers, I said that we weren't sure but as soon as we knew, we would let them know and, of course, they could always follow up and ask again.

I had done a lot of research about the best way to approach this and how to communicate with my kids and my spouse. My hope was that we could handle it in a way that would improve the kids' chances of coming out the other side as well-adjusted, kind, healthy and whole people who could contribute to the world simply by virtue of who they were. I think I can safely say that each of my children is all of those things and more.

The research yielded pretty consistent recommendations. Brian and I were supposed to be open, honest and transparent. We were supposed to communicate and be there for the kids, not to go out every night or even every weekend simply because we were suddenly single. By extension, we weren't supposed to introduce a new significant other too early on. Our primary roles were as parents, and while our relationship with each other might be changing, our parenting should not unless it was to improve. Other recommendations included going to the kids' activities regardless of who had the kids that weekend, to speak positively, or, at the very least, not disparagingly, of the other parent and to not let our moods, arguments, fears or insecurities be imposed upon our children. The last one goes for divorce or no divorce. We wanted to make sure the kids knew how much we loved them and how much we loved being their parents. Finally, we wanted to express that there was nothing the kids did to create the situation just as there was nothing they could do to bring Brian and me back together.

Despite our efforts, and despite approaching the divorce as mindfully as possible, it was still difficult. Difficult for them, difficult for Brian and me and difficult for us as a family. Around that time, I also had to put down our two dogs. Brian and I had gotten them early on in our relationship, so that experience was yet another loss, another goodbye to the life we had built. There were literally days when I could barely get out of bed. I would get the kids off to school and then retreat under the covers until I had to pick them up. Other days, my only saving grace was movement. So I would walk for hours and hours, sometimes with my mom but often alone, just thinking, getting to know myself, learning about who I was and asking myself questions. *What was happening? Why me? Why couldn't I catch a break? What had I done to deserve this? What did I do to cause this?*

What I would realize much later on was that I was asking the wrong questions. I did not yet have the perspective to see that, while the divorce was brutally painful, it was also a gift. I was given this challenge because there was a richer, fuller and better life waiting for all of us. The pain my kids had to go through was almost unbearable for me to witness, especially since I was part of the cause. But I also knew that the dysfunction and toxicity they would experience growing up in a home where their parents were together but no longer in love would be equally damaging, just in a different way. I would never be able to be the mom I wanted to be for them, the mom they deserved, if we lived in that situation.

I had spent about a year agonizing over this decision. The best I could do was to be there for them and provide a strong and solid support system as they navigated their new reality. I spent hours poring over books, videos and podcasts to learn how to get everyone through this, especially the kids. I explored many approaches and cobbled them together to create a plan that worked for me. I also spent a lot of time meditating, immersing myself in my spiritual journey, which allowed me to stay centered, grounded and strong. I communicated openly with my kids and kept them updated as to what was going on as soon as I figured it out and processed it. I tried to hold space for them. Holding space means to walk alongside people in whatever journey they are on without judging them, making them feel inadequate, trying to fix them or trying to impact the outcome. When we hold space for other people, we open our hearts, offer unconditional support and let go of judgment and control. Yes, there was still pain, but I did everything in my power to usher them through that transition in as healthy a way as possible.

My kids have a pretty solid life. I mean, they have the regular challenges that we all face, so the divorce was probably their first major period of adversity. That's why I stayed laser-focused on being intentional about getting through it together in every configuration: me and them, them and their dad and me, them and their dad. I knew the way they experienced this singular, major challenge would lay the groundwork for how they faced other challenges down the road. I wanted to instill a sense of self in them. I wanted them to know they could get through anything that comes up in their lives because they have the tools within themselves. They just need to know how and when to access them. As they stand before me today, two 18-year-old boys and a 16-year-old girl, I am proud to be able to say, "Mission accomplished, Pam! Great job!" These three people are my greatest accomplishments, and if I were to leave Earth tomorrow, I feel confident that they would be more than okay. I am so proud of how they navigated that situation, how they continue to navigate their lives and who they are as human beings. They are very special people.

When going through a divorce with children, I truly believe that we have the power to change the stigma and, more importantly, the power to change the meaning attached to it, the process that is followed, the outcome and how our children are impacted. Once again, it is a choice. In fact, this is true for divorce, career changes and really any major life decision. We have the power to recognize and move beyond our limiting beliefs. I remember when I told my mom that I was going to get divorced, and she counseled me that no one would want to be with a single mom who had three kids. She wasn't trying to be mean. She was honestly trying to help me, but she was coming at it from her own set of limiting beliefs. (Never mind that I wasn't looking for someone else, and never mind that, in the end, she was wrong. There are plenty of men out there who would embrace a relationship with both me and with my kids.) Divorce – or a career change, a move or any other life change – may not be pleasant, but it doesn't have to be awful either.

As I navigated my new, post-divorce reality, I experienced days when I thought I could conquer it all and other days when I wondered what we had done and how life would ever be "normal" again. It wasn't so much that I missed Brian but rather the picture we had created. As I embarked on this new chapter of single-parenthood, it was clear that I would have to step it up in many areas of my life. Aside from parenting, my career had to be a big priority so I could continue to provide the lifestyle we had become accustomed to. How could I combine a successful and demanding career with being a present and active parent for my kids? It was critically important to me to be mentally, emotionally and physically present for my kids at school events, at after-school activities and in the home. In order to make this happen, I believed that the first thing I had to address was *me*. I had to make sure I was as whole a person as I could possibly be so that I had enough to give to others.

Always a lover of anything concerning personal development and growth, I realized I would have to customize my own immersion program, so to speak. I began devouring everything related to improving myself, from books and videos to podcasts. I practiced meditation, yoga, aura cleansings, crystal work and sound therapy. I compiled vision boards, and I began to be more mindful about what I would put in my body, where I directed my attention and who I would allow in my circle and spend time with. I got myself as whole and healthy as I possibly could at that time. It wasn't easy and it took years. But even though I sometimes wished it would happen faster, I could see the progress. That was enough to keep me going. I was leveling up in a big way, and I loved how I was feeling and what it was doing for me.

I can see now how I was going through an awakening. In fact, there would be varying levels of lifting the veil throughout my life. I thought I had arrived, but I had barely even started.

TIPS & TAKEAWAYS

Practicing Self-Love and Self-Care

As I continued to navigate my journey toward my authentic self and experience the highs and lows inherent to that process, I was again smacked in the face with the reality versus the facade. I realized that to get through this next hurdle in life and show up the way I wanted to for myself, my family and those around me, I was going to have to strengthen my inner self. The way I did this was by prioritizing self-love and self-care.

Self-love and self-care look different for everyone, but they always require discipline, self-respect and strength. There are some days when you might not be as on point as others, and that's okay as long as you pick yourself up and get back to it.

Some people still think that self-love and self-care are selfish, but what I have learned is that not practicing these things is actually the selfish act. It's kind of like what they say during the safety drill on the airplane: Put the oxygen mask on yourself before you put it on others.

Self-love and self-care are the same. It's not always easy to do the things that are good for you, but when you work on loving and strengthening yourself, you can offer the best of yourself to those around you and to the world in general.

Begin the journey with these steps:

1. **Go inward**: Don't succumb to the pressure of what you think you should and shouldn't be doing. Get to know yourself, and give yourself time and space to go at your own pace.
2. **Practice gratitude**: Start your day by saying five things you are grateful for before you get out of bed. If it helps, try doing it with another person. My cousin and I send each other a daily text with 10 things we are each grateful for.

3. **Meditate**: Meditation doesn't have to be intimidating or foreign. It can be almost anything that helps you relax, release your energy and center your mind. Traditionally, meditation might include a formal sitting practice, but many people meditate while walking, listening to music, writing, drawing, exercising, practicing yoga, doing any kind of artwork, being in nature, doing the dishes, cleaning, or simply lighting a candle and being in their favorite space.

4. **Don't punish yourself for your choices**: Sometimes we have to make difficult choices that not everyone will understand. That doesn't mean those choices are wrong. Be kind to yourself and be confident that the decisions you make mindfully will set you on the right path.

5. **Practice daily rituals**: In intentionally selecting and practicing specific behaviors, you create powerful connections to the best parts of yourself. These can run the gamut from saying affirmations to taking walks. Other options include taking baths, practicing good skin care, getting massages, reading, listening to podcasts, following meditation programs, exercising, getting outdoors, unplugging for an hour every day, spending time alone, drinking more water and simply eating healthful foods.

CHAPTER 22

Once I had gotten myself as centered as possible, and I could show up the way I wanted to for myself and for my kids, I needed to shift my focus to my career. What was a very successful part-time career had to become an even more financially successful full-time career. Otherwise, I would be forced to make a career change, and I didn't want to do that. I had already determined that real estate offered the most flexibility in terms of a work-life balance. I just needed to figure out how to go from one level to the next.

I knew that I could do this because I had already surpassed my expectations while working in a part-time capacity. But there were still a few unknown variables. Chief among these was the fact that I planned to move forward as a single agent rather than as one half of a partnership. I had learned that while there are lots of amazing benefits to having a partner in business, there are also lots of things that aren't so great. In our case, my friend was still in a part-time frame of mind, and I wanted something bigger. We ended up going our separate ways around the time of my divorce, so I felt like I went through two divorces at once. Not only was I losing my husband, I was also losing one of my closest friends who'd shared in my professional success from the beginning. It was painful for sure, but it was also right. Sometimes you have to get through the storm to see the sun.

One lesson I took away from all this was that if I could survive so much upheaval all at once, there was no way I couldn't handle creating a successful career for myself. And so that's exactly what I did!

I began to research the best of the best in my industry to see what had worked for them. What I learned was that the most successful Realtors all had a plan or a strategy that got them where they wanted to go. So I started to explore various systems designed to help me leverage my professional growth. With the help of a very close friend who had already achieved much higher levels of success as a Realtor than I had, I landed on a program that I thought could be good. It turned out it wasn't just good, it was phenomenal. I signed up that day and decided that I would follow it religiously for six months and then reassess.

There were many things that I loved about that system. One in particular was that it encouraged me to schedule family time into my days and to consider that time as important as an appointment with a client. This was the work-life balance that had won me over to real estate in the first place, and it felt intuitive to formalize one of the industry's most alluring features into my day-to-day experience. So whether it was school events, doctors' visits, dining out, vacations or even just hanging out with my kids, I would put it in my calendar and treat it like any other meeting.

There was a lot of structure to this system as well, which was great since real estate, like most sales positions, doesn't offer any sort of structure on its own. Another similarity between real estate and sales is its mercenary approach to success. At the end of the day, your success (or otherwise) is up to you. If you fail to plan, then you plan to fail!

What happened during those six months was transformative. The only thing I had to reassess at the end of that trial period was to determine how I could do more, do better and go to the next level. This was exciting! My phone was ringing off the hook, and I could not keep up with the business that was coming my way. It was clear that I was on the right track, but I decided that I needed more direction if I were going to level up. That's when I hired a business coach, and it was a decision that became a game changer both personally and professionally. The company that offered the training system I used also featured a coaching division. So my coach specialized in both real estate and the specific system that I was following, and he helped me develop a personalized plan to grow my business exponentially.

Before long, I started to explore what it would look like to build a team and a brand for myself. The idea was twofold: One, a team and a brand identity would leverage my success beyond what I could offer as a single person. Two, in doing so, I could offer leadership, training and leads to other Realtors who weren't experiencing the same level of success that I was. (It's always been important to me to give back, and I am a giver by nature, so this desire was purely instinctual.) I wasn't great at this at the beginning. I thought leadership was about providing direction. Learning to be a good leader, like anything else, was a process. I gradually figured out how to play to each person's strengths and inner resources instead of issuing orders.

I started with a name for my team: The Pam Christian Group. I also started slow and small with one buyer agent and one office administrator. But as my success and confidence grew, so too did my business. This was yet another journey I was embarking on, one that entailed learning, growth, failure, getting back up and repeating it all over again. Eventually, I grew that business to include seven agents and additional support staff. We were one of the top-performing teams in our area. More importantly, our team was recognized as offering the gold standard in real estate, not just in terms of sales but also in service.

One of the biggest lessons I learned from that experience was that you are only as good as the people around you. So the success of my brand had a lot to do with all the people who contributed to the team, and I am forever grateful to them. That includes the ones who didn't work out, because each and every experience taught me something valuable. The Pam Christian Group truly became my fourth child. (Or my fifth if you count the rescue dog my kids and I adopted in 2015!)

As I settled into my new level of success, and as my kids got accustomed to their new normal, I began to focus on my social life. Up until that point, all of my attention went to my kids and my career. I had quickly realized during my divorce that Brian and I could not be friends with the same people. We tried at first, but it turned out most of our joint friends weren't all that trustworthy. They would share with me what Brian had said and vice versa. To me, they weren't worth fighting over or for, and I started to distance myself knowing that my true friends would stay by my side. It was both sad and enlightening that people were so willing to drop me, but the truth was I was just as willing and ready to drop them.

Most days, I loved living alone with my kids, a few close friends and family members, and my work. Some days, it was lonely, and I felt like everyone was talking about me. But mostly I was good with my choice. I genuinely liked myself, so I was okay being alone. Except I wouldn't stay alone for much longer.

TIPS & TAKEAWAYS

Rebuilding

Rebuilding can sound very daunting until you realize we do it all the time. Rebuilding is not exactly starting over but rather refining something – your career, your outlook, yourself – as you move forward. I am constantly rebuilding, even when I am not fully aware of it, and I have been since the first time I was knocked down as a little girl. How does the saying go? One step forward, two steps back? A more fitting expression for rebuilding might be, "One step forward, two leaps ahead." Each time I start to build again, I am not starting from where I was when I was rebuilding the last time. I start from a new place of growth and at a new level with new skills, new strengths and new perspectives – basically a new me – so it isn't daunting but empowering.

When it comes to rebuilding, here is how you can lay the right foundation:

1. **Go at your own pace**: I know I keep mentioning this, but if you need a day to reset, take it. Don't force things! You will have days when you are super motivated. Those are the times when you can go all out. Other days, you may need to rest. Tune in, and let your inner wisdom guide you.

2. **Make a commitment**: Ask yourself: If there were no limits to what you could do, be or have, how would your life look? Promise yourself that you will create such a life without any limits, a life that is designed to make you happy. Don't settle for anything less than you're worth.

3. **Give yourself permission to fail**: Failure is key to growth and rebuilding. We are taught to fear and avoid failure, but mistakes are part of the process. In fact, I learn more from my mistakes than I do from my successes. So release any negative attitudes you have toward failure, and just go for it!

4. **Find your tribe**: Surround yourself with loving people who will support your journey and the new you!

5. **Faith**: Have faith in yourself, the universe, your instincts and your intuition. These things are the foundation upon which everything else is built.

CHAPTER 23

You hear it all the time: You can't love someone else if you don't love yourself. But have you wondered why that is? Truly knowing yourself means understanding what you love about yourself, what you bring to the table and what you need to work on. Only then can you look outward to see what you want from a relationship or another person. And it's important to be aware that this is not a static experience. It is healthy to grow and change and heal, which is why a lot of relationships wind up changing or ending too. But when you find the person who shares the same core values and morals as you (things that don't change) while also embracing self-reflection and personal growth (which cause healthy change), that's when you have found true love, and you should hold on to it with both hands.

As my career began to take off, love entered my life again. I was very close friends with a man I will call Andrew, and our relationship began to grow into a more intimate one. We were best friends first and foremost. He worked in my field, so we had similar backgrounds. As we moved from friends to romantic partners, the relationship grew stormy and intense. It brought out feelings in me that I never knew existed. There were moments of such happiness and love that it essentially blindsided me – I just hadn't known that it was possible to feel like that toward someone else. I was so drawn to him that I wanted to know more. I was so connected to him that his bad days became my bad days; his happiness, my happiness.

Our connection was deep and beautiful, but unfortunately the timing was off. We were both coming off of a divorce and transitioning into our new lives. Perhaps more damningly, we faced some fundamental differences that we just couldn't seem to work through, no matter how hard we tried. I felt far more invested in the relationship than he seemed to be, and while I'm an independent person, I do need some give-and-take. We dated on and off for six years, but in the end, neither of us was ready to meet in the middle and make the necessary adjustments for a successful, long-term relationship.

We decided to take a break in March 2016. A few weeks later, my kids, sister and I went to Costa Rica. On the plane, I met a guy who would make the most unexpected impact on me. He sat near me and we talked a bit during the flight, but I didn't think much of it until we got to the hotel. There, I received an email from him. *How did he get my email address?* I wondered. In his email, he invited me to spend a weekend with him and be his guest at a wedding he was attending in Costa Rica. He said he would take care of all the expenses, and he would get me my own room. Wow! I couldn't tell if this was super romantic or creepy. In the end, I declined the invitation, but we stayed in touch through texts and phone calls for a brief while.

That interlude with this younger guy opened my eyes to the fact that sometimes doors need to close for other doors to open. It showed me that it was time to end, once and for all, my relationship with Andrew. I loved him and wanted it to work, but in holding on to that hope, I was denying myself the possibility of a more fulfilling romantic relationship. Today, Andrew and I are still close friends with a deep love for each other, and I am grateful to have him in my life. I adore his kids and his family and will always have wonderful memories to carry with me.

It's amazing how someone who crossed my path for just a few hours on a plane ride could have such a tremendous impact. But when you are an open person, open to the universe and to the different people you encounter, you receive these clarifying epiphanies. There are no coincidences. Even though it went absolutely nowhere, my experience with that mystery man changed my life.

It was only six weeks later that I met someone new: Sean (as with other names, this one has been changed as well). We bumped into each other at a bodega, and something clicked. I was not looking to get into a relationship – I wasn't ready, and Sean lived an hour away anyway – but he was persistent. We started texting and calling, although we didn't meet up until about six weeks later.

It was an easy relationship. We would occasionally get together, have fun and simply enjoy each other's company. It was refreshing to be in a relationship without drama. Sean came into my life at a pivotal moment. He represented comfort and safety, not only as a ballast to the tempestuous nature of my relationship with Andrew, but also during a very difficult and complicated time in my near future. (More on that in the next chapter.) I knew I wasn't in a place to be in a relationship, but he was just too good to me at a time when I really needed to be taken care of. Usually it is me who is the caretaker and the nurturer, and I like that role. But at that time, I needed someone to do that for me, and Sean was good to me. I enjoyed it, I enjoyed him and I enjoyed the relationship.

I also brought a lot of good to the relationship. I helped Sean grow in ways he couldn't have imagined possible for himself. I encouraged him to switch careers when he was miserable in his current position, and I helped him learn how to communicate better with his former wife so he could have a better relationship with her and with his kids. But I knew from day one that it wouldn't last. The spark was missing, the passion. At first, I figured it was just the drama that was missing. After all, everything I had ever experienced or had modeled for me in the way of romantic relationships seemed to involve high-level drama. So I thought this stable, loving and comforting relationship might be the natural antidote to the previous dysfunction, and I stuck it out to see what it could be like.

I was upfront with Sean from the very beginning too. I knew he was more emotionally invested than I was, and I wanted to be transparent. I think he thought something would change for me, like a switch would flip, but it didn't. During the course of that three-year relationship, I did a lot of self-reflection on how I view relationships. Eventually, I realized that you can be in a relationship without drama, and that is definitely a non-negotiable for me today. My other non-negotiable, however, is that there be that spark and passion, not just comfort. My relationship with Sean was safe, and he was a sweet and super-attentive guy for whom I wish nothing but the best, and who I am glad crossed my path. But he was not the one.

TIPS & TAKEAWAYS

In Love With Love

Wow! I can go on and on about this one. I am a lover of all things pertaining to love and truly believe in the ultimate love story. What I don't believe in is the way love is so often portrayed in our culture. Love is not attachment. It is not ownership. It does not have terms or conditions. It should not be forced. It should not be sought just because you are lonely or want to check off the "love" box. And, most of all, it is not meant to complete you – that's your job and no one else's.

To me, love should be free flowing and easy. It represents an open heart that sends the frequency of love everywhere. It means holding space for someone and meeting that person where he or she is, not where you are. Most importantly, love is inspiring and supporting your partner to be the best version of himself or herself possible. We all have flaws. It comes down to looking within yourself and deciding what you are okay with in a partner rather than trying to get someone to change to meet your needs. It's loving someone as is.

Invite love into your life with these steps:

1. **Keep an open heart**: Everyone is different. Each person you meet has different baggage and triggers as well as something different to offer you, so don't write off love just because of some bad experiences.

2. **Lay the groundwork for love to find you**: You have to make sure you're happy in your life in general before you try to find happiness in a relationship, and sometimes that means doing the work to learn how to love yourself first. For example, it was through that process of working on myself, of rediscovering who I was and gaining confidence in the process, that love found me. I was never really looking for it, but it arrived on my journey of healing.

3. **Heal**: Learn your patterns and triggers, so you can work through them, or they will continue to impact your relationships.

4. **Relinquish the pursuit of perfection**: The sooner you understand that there is no such thing as the perfect guy, girl or relationship, the better.

5. **Spread love**: Love goes well beyond relationships. Send out love to the world with kindness. It's like planting seeds – in sharing love through kindness, love comes back to you in all forms.

6. **Follow your heart**: Don't let society's rules get in the way. True love sees past any man-made obstacle, whether it's race, age, different backgrounds or any other construct that our culture has created.

7. **Find your love language**: Everyone has their own way of showing affection or expressing love. For one person, it might be giving gifts. For another, it might be spending time together. No one love language is better than another

or indicative of someone being more or less in love. Embrace the differences, and get to know which languages you and your partner gravitate toward. The sooner you each understand how to express and receive love together, the smoother and more harmonious your relationship will be.

CHAPTER 24

Around the time Sean and I met in spring of 2016, my mom, sister and I began to notice that my dad's health was deteriorating. The issues primarily affected his vision, which came as no surprise. He had suffered from a condition called retinitis pigmentosa (RP) since he was in his mid-30s. RP is a group of disorders that causes the breakdown of cells in the retina, which then affects how the retina responds to light. It causes tunnel vision to the point of blindness – your peripheral vision gradually disappears until you can no longer see at all. When he was diagnosed, my dad was told it was just a matter of time before he would be legally blind. During the 40-plus years following his diagnosis, he lost all of his peripheral vision, his visual world narrowing with every piece that disappeared, and he no longer drove, which was a devastating blow to him. But with his characteristic strength and determination, my dad also challenged the inevitable. He and my mom joined the board of the Foundation Fighting Blindness and even founded the organization's annual Vision Walk held at chapters across the country. And while he struggled with the disease, constantly bumping into people and things so that he had bruises everywhere, his deterioration progressed slower than it would have without the cutting-edge treatments he tried. So when he told us he was experiencing blurry vision and headaches, the first stop was his eye doctor. We had no idea that these and other symptoms pointed toward a different illness altogether.

As he and my mom went from doctor appointment to doctor appointment trying to figure out what was going on, I was adapting to single life yet again while also enjoying having Sean to connect with occasionally. Life was pretty good. The kids and I spent Mother's Day with my parents that year. My dad definitely looked worn out, but we had an amazing day together. We spent it the way we often did with a couple of hours in their apartment, a walk through Central Park, a little time in the playground that my kids grew up going to and then a walk by the bench that my parents donated in my kids' names. We always like to stop by that bench when we are in the city. It resides in a prime location in Central Park with a beautiful plaque that reads, "IN JOYOUS CELEBRATION OF OUR WONDERFUL GRANDCHILDREN MICHAEL, ALEXANDER AND JESSICA – GRANDMA AND PAPA."

After that day, I saw my dad just one more time before the call came in the early hours of May 17, 2016. I remember waking up that morning, the illusion of normalcy shattered as I checked my phone and saw several missed calls from my sister. As soon as I reached her, she delivered the bad news. "Pam," she said, "we are in the emergency room. Dad fell out of bed around 3 a.m. and couldn't get up. We're at Lenox Hill now." She suggested I get to the city ASAP and bring the kids. That was the part that shook me. Everyone who knows me knows how protective I am of what my kids are exposed to. (They were in sixth and eighth grade by that time.) So my sister telling me to bring them to the hospital and miss school put me in full panic mode. This could not be good.

I woke everyone up, and we headed into the city. My mom and sister, who lived a few blocks away from each other, were in the emergency room as we entered. There was nothing that could've prepared me to see the man lying on the hospital bed in front of me, and there is no amount of time that will remove that image from my mind. The strong, dominant man who always loomed large, whom

I both feared and loved, was unrecognizable. He was in and out of consciousness and, as I made my way over to him, I tried to process what was going on but my brain just wasn't keeping up. What had happened to cause my dad to shrivel up just days after celebrating Mother's Day together? My mom and sister, who had been in the ER with my dad since the early morning, were worn out and couldn't see what I saw: He was clearly slipping away in front of our eyes. I knew something had to be done immediately or we were going to lose him.

I am so glad I listened to my sister and brought my kids to the hospital that day. Their voices helped rouse my dad back into consciousness for a few moments, and I was able to have each of them give him a kiss and enjoy their own moment with him during that brief interlude of lucidity. After that, I felt the best thing would be to get them back to school so I could focus on the next steps for my dad. I wanted to be there for my mom and team up with my sister to do whatever needed to be done. I called a friend to pick up the kids, told each of them that I loved them so much and then, after they left, I took charge. I immediately told my mom and sister that if Dad were to stay in the emergency room, we were going to lose him. It was time to take action.

The medical system is an innovative, complicated and sometimes straight-up dysfunctional beast. You have to learn its language if you are going to effectively advocate for someone who is hospitalized. My family was fortunate. We had access to people and resources who could help us get my dad to the "right" doctor. What about everyone else? What happens when you don't have the right insurance or any insurance? What happens when you don't know which questions to ask, which requests to make?

My mom stayed with our dad while my sister and I headed outside to find better phone service. We started furiously making calls. At last, we were able to connect with some people we knew who then cut through all the red tape and got my dad transferred out of the ER and onto one of the floors where he could get more attention. This was the kind of attention he deserved, the kind of attention we *all* deserve!

Our first choice was to move my dad to one of the floors that offered hotel-like accommodations, but we were informed that he was too sick. The kind of care he needed would require him to be on a floor for more serious conditions. What?! "Serious" conditions?! What were they talking about?! Before we could fully panic, we made it to my dad's room and found him slowly regaining consciousness. We caught glimpses of him coming through the shell and gradually started talking to him as he became more alert. Then his medical team arrived and, after introductions, informed us the next step was to identify a diagnosis and treatment protocol.

We quickly realized that there were not a lot of options for treatment plans when we were greeted in the hallway by the palliative-care team. Palliative care! I must, I thought, be hearing things or not know what this means, because I was always under the impression that palliative care referred to making people as comfortable as possible as they transition out of this life. That couldn't be though. I was completely blindsided, and yet I should have known all along. In 1999, my dad had been diagnosed with prostate cancer and non-Hodgkin lymphoma, but he had been in remission for at least a decade. Over the past month, he hadn't been feeling well, and his vision was distorted and blurry. Since he had RP, he was visiting eye specialists thinking that his symptoms were connected to that. What we found out, however, was that those new vision symptoms and some other issues he was having were actually caused by central nervous system lymphoma and related complications. Central nervous system lymphoma is a rare, non-Hodgkin lymphoma in which cancer cells from the lymph tissue form in the brain and/or spinal cord. The way the doctors described it to us was even more evocative. It was, they said, like an explosion in the brain. We were told that with steroids he only had four to six weeks to live, and the steroids were really meant for the family's benefit. They would buy us time to say our goodbyes.

It just seemed so sudden that we had no time to even process that he was sick, let alone dying. We were scared, sad, angry, motivated and task-oriented. We were determined to do everything possible for our dad so he could beat this! So we started casting about for options. We contacted the organization The Truth About Cancer and many other leading holistic practitioners to see if there were other options out there. We looked into hyperbaric chambers and facilities out of the country that were not bound by FDA rules and regulations. The only issue we kept bumping into was that our dad was not ambulatory. He was, in other words, too weak to travel. So it was back to the drawing board. Because his condition was extremely rare, there were only two local doctors who specialized in treating it. One was at Hackensack University Medical Center and one was at Columbia. We chose Columbia because we liked the doctor, and my mom and sister both lived in the city. (While my sister had a demanding career, she didn't have kids and so she had a certain level of freedom that I didn't.)

The following weeks were a blur peppered by experiences I still remember vividly. One of these happened when I came to visit at a time when my sister wasn't there. I walked into the room and found my mom sleeping in the small, twin-size hospital bed with her arms wrapped around my dad. She literally stayed by his side every single day while he was hospitalized. It was devastating and beautiful to watch at the same time. They had been together longer than they had been on their own as individuals, and I wondered how my mom would do on her own without her beloved.

As a single mom, I was used to everything revolving around my kids and being on a tight schedule so that things ran smoothly. But during this time, our orbit needed to shift to revolve around my dad. As my boys wrapped up their last days of middle school, I was making a daily drive to and from New York City. Finally, I took my kids to see my dad for what would be the last time one Saturday morning that May. Because my kids had never experienced anything like this before, I gave them plenty of background on what was going on, what Papa looked like and what to expect. Unfortunately, I neglected to give myself the same preparation. We walked into my dad's room. It was bright but cold, the energy low and somber. My dad's typically booming voice had inexplicably dropped to barely a whisper, even before his hospitalization. But as soon as he saw his grandchildren, his face lit up.

The kids were amazing as always. They truly rose to the occasion, despite being out of their comfort zone. I mean, who wouldn't be? As they started to discuss the basketball playoffs, I decided to leave them alone to chat. I watched them through the small window in the door to make sure they were okay, and I started to sob. I knew that this would be the last time my kids would see my dad on this earth, and that was a very hard pill to swallow. Even writing this now makes me cry. My dad was so proud and elated to be a grandpa; he adored his grandkids. He made up for many of the mistakes he'd made as a dad when he became a grandfather, and he was able to express himself in ways he had never been able to do with me as his daughter. It was deeply touching and devastating that, at 14 and 12 years old, my kids were making their final memories with their beloved Papa. My dad was such a huge force and presence in our lives. How could this be happening? It was all too much to process.

We spent weeks at the hospital. My dad had originally wanted hospice at home. He wanted to sit in his office – his very favorite space in the apartment that he had designed so many years ago. But when he found out there might be a chance that he could buy some real time with the progressive doctor and treatment at Columbia, he changed his mind and decided to pursue that avenue. He wanted to live just a little longer and was willing to try, but he was also very clear that if this innovative treatment did not work, then that was it. He did not want to try any other options. He said he would want to pass in his favorite chair in his library in the comfort of his own home.

Our next step was to get him over to Columbia University Irving Medical Center, and the ambulance ride took its toll. By the time we got to his room at Columbia, he looked the same as when he had been admitted to the Lenox Hill emergency room. His speech was slurred, his skin was sagging, he couldn't stand on his own and he was edgy and irritable. (Well, actually, that part was par for the course.) We tried to make his room more comfortable, adding belongings and crystals from home, diffusing essential oils and bringing nutrient-dense food so he wasn't eating what the hospital had to offer. But even with all of our efforts, we were losing him. His new doctor explained that my dad had to get stronger and healthier before he could begin the new treatment.

After maybe nine days, he was able to start the treatment, but we had a couple of scares. I remember one day I got the call that I had to get to the city immediately because we were losing him. I drove in praying that I would make it in time to say goodbye only to arrive at the garage near the hospital and find a long line of cars in front of me. I got out of the car, screaming that my dad was about to die, and I wanted to see him before he did, could someone please take care of my car. Then I left. I ran the two blocks to the hospital hoping to make it in time to see him alive. I made it – and so did he. I realized that I would need to say goodbye each time I left, because there was no guarantee that there would be another opportunity.

Then the day came when my sister called to say, "Pam – Dad stopped breathing, and they need our permission to intubate him." What did this mean? I mean, I knew what it meant on an intellectual level, but what did it mean for him and our family? The doctors explained that we could lose him quickly if we did not put in a breathing tube, so together, my mom, sister and I agreed. I hurried into the city and ran to my dad's room. (I could always find his room by following my nose: Every day, we would diffuse different essential oils.) The doctors were rolling him out to go to the ICU because he'd lost consciousness. I held his hand, gave him a kiss and told him that I loved him and would meet him down there.

He would never regain consciousness. For the next several days, he remained in the ICU, and we were by his side every single day.

I remember one poignant moment in particular. My dad loved the singer Josh Groban and found his music very touching. We all knew his favorite song and pulled it up on one of our phones.

Holding hands with each other and with my dad, we all stood around him, singing along to that song. It might sound a bit odd, but it was one of many beautiful moments that we had over the last three days of my dad's life.

My dad went into the hospital on May 17, 2016. Just three weeks later, on June 5, 2016, he took his last breath. He was 73 years old. The days following my dad's passing were consumed by tasks. It was a surreal experience where time seemed to drag even as the days flew by. Plans for the funeral needed to be made, people informed and a eulogy written. The last of these fell to me. I appreciated the task of delivering the eulogy, because I recognized it as an opportunity to honor him. That was a gift.

In the end, his funeral was standing-room only. It was like a greatest hits of his life with people from all parts of his past arriving to pay their respects, including two men from the U.S. military who played taps and presented my mom with an American flag ceremonially folded 13 ways. It was beautiful. I wanted to be true to my dad's character, good and bad, and I spoke from the heart. People laughed and cried and, I think, understood the man we were there to remember.

While I will always wish we had more time together in this life, I will forever cherish the time we did have. What he taught me – both what I wanted to model and what I wanted to do differently – was invaluable. I am so grateful for his impact on my life.

TIPS & TAKEAWAYS

Seize the Day!

Although life had always been difficult for me, I never thought I would experience something as devastating as the loss of a parent so early in my life. True, I wasn't in my teens or even in my 30s, but most of my friends still had their parents, and I just expected my dad to be around for a very long time. I expected him to share in my kids' milestones with me, as he was as proud a grandfather as I have ever seen. He was invincible in my mind.

Just as I once thought divorce was something that happened to other people (until I went through one myself), I was of the mindset that losing a close family member happened to other people, but not to our family and not to me. So when I was faced with my dad's mortality, and as I watched my mom shepherd him through his last weeks, I learned a lot. I learned so much about love and devotion. Most of all, I learned never to take anything for granted but to live each day to the fullest.

I kind of thought that that lesson might wear off as so many do when we get back to "life," but my dad's absence has been so profound that the opposite has happened. His laugh, his nicknames for me (Pam Pam, Sweet Potato, Shining Eyes, Princess), his generosity, his business savvy, his ability to bring out the best (and sometimes the worst) in others, his determination, his strength, his ferocity and his all-consuming love, admiration and loyalty for his family – all of this will live in me forever. So while the loss has devastated me, it has not defeated me. It has made me rise up. It has made me fight even harder, and it has made me live each and every day to the fullest, whatever that means to me on a given day. And that is the best way I could ever honor my dad.

Embracing the beauty and challenge of the present starts with the following:

1. **Be in the moment**: This moment is all we ever have, so you might as well enjoy it while you are here. Stop sleepwalking through life!

2. **Let people know how you feel about them**: Don't be too shy, fearful of rejection or embarrassed. Tell people what they mean to you while you have the chance.

3. **Live the life you want**: Life is short, so stop procrastinating. Figure out what you want to do and go for it. Don't let your limiting beliefs hold you back for another second!

4. **Live in alignment with your purpose**: Do something every day that feeds your soul. For example if you like giving back, start by giving a stranger a compliment. It will change that person's day as well as yours!

CHAPTER 25

The year that followed my dad's passing was a blur. I was grieving while being pulled in different directions – my kids, my mom and my career all needed and deserved my attention. I was stressed out and on autopilot as I ran all over the place trying to accommodate everyone's needs. I was gaining weight as a result, and experiencing the symptoms of grief and stress, including digestive issues, fatigue, lowered immunity and mild depression. It felt horrible.

I wasn't the only one hurting. After losing her husband, best friend, dictator and guide, my mom began to go through the various stages of grief. At first, she seemed unusually upbeat and okay, almost as if she felt liberated. She was devastated, yes, but she had spent weeks in the hospital with my dad (she left only once), and before that, she'd spent years taking care of him. And trust me, that was not easy. After that initial shock, she came down with a nasty cold that she couldn't shake, which was followed by situational depression. It was November by that point. Winter had set in, and my mom's illness and depression had stripped her of her usual energy, leaving her tired and with no appetite. Since she was already petite, the weight that she lost left her looking unwell, a shell of herself. I began to really worry about her; she was lonely and missing her partner.

As she began to emerge from the depression the following spring, anger took its place. Anger at him for leaving her, anger at him for all the years she allowed him to bully her and anger that she was left alone when they were just beginning this new stage of their lives. While anger can be an uncomfortable feeling, my mom was working through it in a healthy way, and she was making progress. At least it seemed this way.

For as long as I can remember, my mom and I spoke on the phone at least once a day, and usually it was a lot more than that. So, when I didn't hear from her one evening, I assumed she fell asleep early, which wasn't unusual for her at that point. She was weak both physically and emotionally, so she often got into bed early. The next day, she was supposed to meet up with my sister, but my sister called me to say she hadn't heard from our mom regarding their plans. This was extremely uncharacteristic of my mom. I was supposed to see her the next day as it was my birthday, but something wasn't sitting right with me. So I suggested my sister go to my mom's place and make sure everything was okay.

It was June 17, 2017. As my sister walked the two blocks between their apartments, she and I chatted on the phone. The sun was warm in the brilliant blue sky, the birds were singing – it was a beautiful, vivid day. My sister stepped into the elevator and said she would go into the apartment, check everything out and call me back. We hung up, and I waited anxiously for her call. Suddenly, the phone rang.

"Hello?" I answered.

"Pam," my sister replied, "she's dead."

I felt that plummeting sensation of dread, as if all the color and life were suddenly drained from my body. I had to catch my breath, I had to compose myself and be there for my sister who was understandably shaken. I was on the phone with the police when my sister called me back, so I let her call go to voicemail. As soon as I got off with the police, Sean called me. I told him I couldn't talk, but he already knew what had happened and offered to make the hourlong drive to my side of town and help any way I needed. (Apparently, when her call had gone to my voicemail, my sister called Sean and asked him to make sure I hadn't fainted.) I got my kids together not knowing what to say to them. I told them Grandma wasn't doing well, and I needed to head into the city. By that point, they were used to the appointments and scheduling happening around my mom, so after a few questions, I was on my way.

I drove into the city in complete shock. I remember calling a few people to help me process what was happening and to help me get through the ride into the city. *Was this really happening? I mean, what the…? How could this be my reality?*

Finally, I arrived at my parents' building, and I was greeted by the doorman I had known almost my entire life. I could hardly breathe. *What was happening?* I got into the elevator and, for the first time in all the years we lived in the building, I wished that the elevator opened to a hallway instead of their apartment so I could have more time. But then there was no amount of time that would prepare me for what I had to walk into.

The elevator doors parted to reveal a sea of police officers. My sister was talking with one of them when our eyes connected. She introduced me to the police investigator, who began to ask me a series of questions. As the line of inquiry became more specific, it dawned on me that the police had to investigate the possibility of foul play. The sudden nature of my mom's death and the way she was found suggested the possibility that her passing was not due to natural causes. Of course, this was beyond upsetting. I interrupted the investigator to say, "I want to see my mom." He said he was sorry but that I couldn't do that right now. I started crying, and thankfully he had some compassion. He said the only way I could see her was if he went with me.

We walked into my dad's office, the room where my dad had so desperately wanted to spend his last days but wasn't able to, and I found my mom lying on the ground. That image will be etched in my brain forever. She was lying in blood and yet as lovely as ever. Oh my beautiful, special mom. My mom who had been by my side every day, with whom I spoke and texted multiple times a day. My mom who never gave up on me. *How could this be happening? Why? Why? Why? Why did life have to be so hard?*

Suddenly, something shifted, and I pulled myself together. I had to compose myself and handle this the way my parents would have expected me to. I decided I would focus on the emotions of this later – when I drove home, when I got home, when I had my own space – but at that very moment, my sister and I needed to take care of and honor our mom.

So much of what followed was out of our hands, but one of the first things my sister and I could do was call two close family friends who had supported us through our dad's passing just a year earlier and who we knew would stand by us during this traumatic time as well. Then we spent the next day, my 43rd birthday, calling friends, relatives and loved ones to deliver the news. It was surreal. We were essentially doing this all over again, just one year after our dad's passing. The difference was that we had to plan a funeral with none of the parental support we'd had the last time, and we had to do it while we were in the middle of a police investigation that we were told would take a month. During that time, we would not have access to the apartment.

So my sister and I began planning as best we could, relying on our family friends and what we remembered from planning our dad's funeral. Once again, I had the gift of delivering the eulogy, this time for an amazing woman who had touched and inspired so many. She was a champion for those who struggled. She served organizations like the enCourage Kids Foundation, which facilitates programs for critically, chronically and terminally ill children. You know the Fun Centers on the pediatric wards of so many hospitals? My mom and dad were instrumental in implementing those in order to make the hospital experience just a little easier for those kids.

My mom's work spanned a range of causes, including a program that supported mental health for veterans and The Doe Fund, a nonprofit organization that matches work, housing and education with people who have histories of homelessness, incarceration or substance abuse.

My mom's impact on the people she worked with was visible the day we held her funeral. In addition to her friends and family, people from all the organizations where she had dedicated her time and energy arrived to celebrate her memory. People contacted my sister and me for months after the funeral to share with us the ways our mom had affected their lives. One of the most moving examples of this came from the people at Al-Anon, where my mom had spent several years getting the support and perspective she needed after my dad had relapsed. Her group there decided to arrange a private memorial for her and invited my sister and me to share in it, which was a tremendous honor considering the confidential nature of the group.

Following the funeral, my sister and I would have typically welcomed family and friends into my parents' apartment to pay their respects and grieve together. We had done this for my dad, but this time, the police investigation was underway and we had to find an alternative. This only made things more difficult – we wanted to grieve with loved ones amid the warmth and comfort of our childhood home. In the end, we reserved a hotel ballroom. It wasn't ideal, but it was the best we could do in that situation.

As it turned out, the police investigation only took a week. It was determined that my mom had died from hemorrhaging after falling and hitting her head.

My sister and I grappled with the shock and stress of our loss. How could two people with such a huge presence in our lives no longer exist? How would I possibly go on without my best friend? How could I move forward without the two people who had championed me my entire life (even if it wasn't always in the most productive way)? I couldn't believe that it was pretty much just me and my sister now. Thank goodness for her!

I found it a little harder to process my mom's death than my dad's, because her passing was so abrupt. I also had PTSD after finding her like that. I remember having a hard time leaving my kids alone at home afterward, fearing that the house would burn down or the kids would be hurt while I was gone. Usually, you have in the back of your mind that such things are possible, but you also know they are unlikely. Yet, with my mom's passing, that veneer of safety peeled away from my life. Suddenly, I would come home after running an errand, and it not only seemed possible but all too real that one of my kids might've been hurt while I was gone. That was some serious trauma I had to work through, which I did with the help of a trusted professional. But I took comfort in knowing that neither my mom nor I left anything unsaid. We were always very open about our feelings for each other, and even more so in the year after my dad died. My mom knew exactly how I felt about her, how much I loved and appreciated her, how much I respected her and how grateful I was for her impact on our family and on the world in general. And I knew exactly how my mom felt about me. It's funny how life works. Just two months before she passed away, my mom got up during a celebration for my daughter and spoke not about Jessica but about me and how she felt toward me. I watch the video from that day every year. It was the best gift she could have ever left me with.

I was kinder to myself after my mom passed away. I spent a lot of time alone. I allowed myself to feel it, to be in it, to embody it. While I'd had to be there for my mom when my dad passed, I decided to put myself first this time. Of course, I was there for my kids, but with everything else, I set boundaries and took the time I needed, and I am grateful that I did. I spent a lot of time in isolation. I was scared. I was scared of what was next; I was soul-searching, trying to figure out my path. And I was trying to work through the thoughts and memories that would flash through my mind from the years with my parents. It was during this time that I realized I wanted something deeper and more meaningful in my life. The question was: What would that look like?

TIPS & TAKEAWAYS

Grieving

At this point, you would think that loss and grief would be familiar to me, right? Like long-lost friends? But grief is one of those funny things that, no matter how many times you have wrestled with it in the past, it feels fresh every time you encounter it. It can come on just as strong, it can hit you out of nowhere and it can come in waves. It can disappear for a while, so you think it's gone for good, only to have it reappear with no notice.

You see, grief is not just about death. Lots of things can cause grief: sexual, physical and verbal abuse; divorce; loss of health; loss of a job; miscarriage; loss of financial stability; loss of a friend; loss of a cherished dream; loss of a pet; loss of safety after trauma; and so much more.

I experienced a lot of loss in my life, and I grieved, even when I didn't recognize it as such. I grieved the loss of the little girl I was and the life that I could have had if it hadn't been stolen from me. I grieved friendships that came and went. I grieved the white-picket-fence life that I once had. And, of course, I grieved the loss of my mom and dad and so many other things along the way.

With each loss, the grieving process looked different, but it was always impactful and important to my healing. Our natural instinct is to run away from pain, but avoiding it just keeps you in an endless loop of pain. You have to face it and feel it in order to move on.

Here is where to start:

1. **Acknowledge your grief**: Trying to ignore grief won't make it go away. In fact, trying to avoid it usually only succeeds in making it emerge in a more toxic way. For real healing, it's important to face your grief and deal proactively with it.

2. **Grieving is personal**: Everyone grieves in their own way. Be kind to yourself, and resist the pressure to act a certain way or finish by a certain time.

3. **Take care of yourself**: You have been wounded. Give yourself some extra TLC and let yourself heal. Make sure that you eat nourishing food, that you exercise, that you get enough rest and that you give yourself a break.

4. **Establish a simple routine**: Having a basic routine will help keep you focused and provide structure during a difficult time. Your day could be as simple as getting out of bed at the same time every day, brushing your teeth, taking a shower, grabbing some water, walking your dog and taking care of one or two things on your to-do list. Don't complicate it or put too much on your plate.

5. **Scale back your obligations**: Unfortunately, life doesn't stand still when we are grieving. But we do have ways to lighten the load. Reach out to trusted friends and loved ones and ask for help, whether you need a shoulder to lean on, someone to go to the grocery store for you or even coverage at work.

6. **Notice the red flags**: When grief begins to feel more like depression, or when you engage in unhealthy coping strategies or self-destructive behaviors (e.g., overconsumption of drugs, alcohol or food; constant sleeping), seek out professional help or support from trusted loved ones.

CHAPTER 26

Following our mom's passing, my sister and I were truly on overload. There were so many tasks and emotions to process, from selling our parents' home, to learning and managing our dad's businesses, to grieving for the loss of both of them.

What was especially surreal during those two years of repeated trauma was that, in between the caretaking and the wrapping up of loose ends, I still had to manage and maintain my other life. My life as a single mom with three kids. My life as a top Realtor with many pending transactions and people relying on me in a declining market.

Prior to my dad's passing, I had been toying with the idea of a career switch. For 15 years, I had given 120 percent of myself to my clients and my industry. And while I loved being a Realtor, while I loved my clients, my colleagues and my industry as a whole, I was craving something more.

I had to put that feeling on hold during those two years of loss. When I reemerged, I was more certain than ever that I was ready to move on to a new career. Real estate had been amazing to me, but it had also run its course. What was I meant to do next? Nothing resonated with me, and I was feeling out of alignment. This emotional upheaval was reflected physically too. I had gained a lot of weight during that time, and I knew that was affecting me. It wasn't so much about how the extra weight looked on me, it was how it made me feel inflamed, unhealthy and low energy – just not myself. I could not continue like this. Something had to change, but...where to start?

I had invested 12 years in building my business, and I wanted to figure out a way to maintain a passive income from it even after I sold it. In the end, I was able to do exactly that. I packaged it as best I could, given the circumstances, and I received a bunch of offers, which was exciting, validating and a relief. I ultimately went with someone who I thought would do a great job with my clients.

I thought there might be another kind of grief and loss associated with selling my business, but I actually felt unburdened. I decided to focus on what was most important to me: my kids, getting my parents' affairs in order and healing myself. I was finishing up active real estate transactions, and other Realtors started calling me, asking if I would coach them in the business. Now that everyone knew I was leaving real estate, I think people felt more comfortable approaching me to learn more about my strategies. So business was picking up on that end without me even trying.

I took a full year off before I stepped into my next role. That year was not intentional. It just sort of happened, and it was one of the most beautiful, uncomfortable, scary, sad, grief-stricken, wonder-filled, eye-opening years of my entire life. At first, I struggled with the lack of structure, the lack of purpose and the downtime, even while I instinctively understood that it was what I needed. It wasn't the right time to jump into anything, much as I wanted to. So my day went from being a hands-on mom and CEO of my top-performing team to looking for ways to fill my time. My kids were older and didn't need me in the same way, there was no more team to run, and it was just me and my thoughts for most of the day.

I constantly wondered how I would get through each day and what I could do to find my purpose. I would spend most of the time reflecting and listening to that inner voice guiding me. What I kept coming back to was this calling to help people. I just wasn't sure how. I thought about fostering a child, but it wasn't the right time. I thought about launching a wellness center. I thought about a lot of things and eventually landed on coaching and motivational speaking. Coaching is a natural extension of what I have done my whole life. My mission is to help heal humanity by inspiring and motivating others to live their best lives.

While I was exploring my options, I started writing this book. It started as a way to heal, and I wasn't sure where it would lead or if I would even publish it. But I decided to keep going and see where it took me, and I'm so glad I did.

What all this leads me to realize is that rest, recovery and reflection are essential parts of the progress toward a successful and happy life; at least they are for me.

Today, I stand before you as a whole human being. I am strong and empowered; I am humble and curious. I am doing what I love, which is the one thing that has always come naturally to me: taking care of people and guiding them the same way I guided that broken little girl out of the deep hole she was plunged into. Because of what I have been through, I am a richer and more textured human being. I am so grateful to have lived the life I have and to be living the life I am now. I am grateful for each person I have met on the journey – everyone becomes a piece of the fabric of who we are. It was not easy in any way, shape or form. It was anything but safe. But it has been full and colorful and all my own.

Even though I may have wanted it to happen faster, and even though I may not have always known it was happening, I can see now how my growth has been a slow and steady process, a constant in the background of my sometimes chaotic life. I have truly lived life to the fullest, and I want that for you too. I've come to realize that the worst times in my life created the best parts of me, and it can be that way for you as well. You have to allow the pain to push you out of your comfort zone so you can search for answers and healing rather than sitting in all that suffering as you hope and wait for it to be over. It is time to remove the veil. It is time to open our eyes to what is ours to enjoy and ours to embrace.

TIPS & TAKEAWAYS

Learning to Forgive

At some point, I realized the only way to move forward in life is to let go, and one of the biggest components of letting go is forgiveness. Throughout so much of my life, I was full of sadness, fear, heartbreak, pain, humiliation, shame, anxiety, guilt and anger. I couldn't carry that with me forever. So I started by forgiving my parents and understanding that they did the best they could with the tools they had. I recognized that it wasn't a lack of love that prevented them from doing better. It was their own limitations. There was no question that they loved me very much and wanted the best for me.

Then I worked on forgiving my abuser. I needed to forgive him in order to move on. To this day, people still ask me how I could forgive what is essentially unforgivable. I usually respond with, "How could I not?" I wanted to end my suffering, and forgiving him was a key factor to accomplishing that. Forgiveness isn't about letting someone else off the hook; it's about freeing the forgiver.

I continued to forgive the people who I felt had "wronged" me. I also asked for forgiveness from those I knew I had hurt or wronged. Sometimes this meant giving them a call, writing a note or sending a message. Other times, the person wasn't in a place to accept or extend the forgiveness. That was okay. Just the effort of reaching out and trying to make amends works, because it's about what you give, not what you get back. In fact, forgiveness often has nothing to do with the other person. It's more about the peace it affords you.

While it was not easy or quick (it is a process that has taken years), forgiveness is a key part of healing. But there was more. I wasn't sure what the more was until I looked deep within and realized there was one person I hadn't yet forgiven: me.

In recent years, I have shown myself even more love and compassion and recognized that I deserve to be happy. I have forgiven myself, and I continue to forgive myself because basic, everyday life happens. We make mistakes. Other people make mistakes. It's easy to find reasons to be angry, hurt and bitter, but I don't want to live in that space. So for me, forgiveness is part of my everyday life, and it will be for the rest of my life.

Find your path to forgiveness with the following steps:

1. **Recognize that you're telling a story that can be changed**: You can continue to be the victim, or you can take control and change the narrative.
2. **Focus on empathy**: Empathy for the other person and empathy for yourself. There is value in not only understanding how the other person feels but in self-empathy as well, a concept centered on the belief that, as a human being, you are inherently worthy of compassion and kindness.
3. **Feel it**: Feel it, process it and let it go.
4. **Moving on to the next act**: There's good stuff ahead. By continually reliving what you went through and not forgiving yourself or someone else, you are trapping yourself in a toxic cycle that will only hold you back from living your best life.

AFTERWORD

In 2005, I received a letter from my dad. He'd written it while he and my mom were on a trip to Israel. There, my dad had engaged in moments of deep reflection, which led to a sense of clarity about his and my relationship. He understood the damage that had been done to me and his part in it, and in this letter, he took responsibility. His ability to see what he had done and to own his mistakes was inspiring. I know it couldn't have been easy for him to put that down on paper. And although I had already forgiven both him and my mother on my own, that letter helped reestablish a trust that led to a more loving relationship between us.

Even though my dad and I never discussed this letter (there was still too much shame around the abuse for me to talk about it), there was an unspoken burden lifted from our relationship. That allowed us to strengthen our bond. And amid the hurt, the pain and the damage, the bond is truly what it is all about.

I now know that the pain my dad caused me was only a reflection of the pain he was in himself. Most of all, I know that it was never personal and that he never wanted to cause me pain.

I have read that letter many times over the years. I wish I had told him while he was alive how much I appreciated his words, his concern and his taking responsibility, but I just couldn't bring myself to say the words. I am sure he knows, though. We talk all the time, and I have told him over and over again.

That letter was and continues to be hugely important to me. What it has taught me is that we can't shy away from the hard conversations with the people we love, and that is especially true in parent-child relationships. You may not get the response you want the first, the second or even the third time, but you've planted the seeds when you dare to discuss the things that are uncomfortable or scary to you. Don't ever give up on the parent-child relationship. It might not be perfect. You might not even like your parent or child. But that relationship is one of the most important ones you will ever have. You have to keep on fighting for it.

Here is the letter that my dad wrote, with key names blacked out:

6/x/05 Tel Aviv
Israel

Dearest Pom Pom,

You have suffered the worst trauma a young child could experience, your ██████████ actions and your DAD NOT BEING There to Believe and support you. No wonder your childhood was so difficult. And to that my Behavior and lack of tenderness, just when you needed it most, is a major fortune on my Behalf. I can never forgive myself for your lost childhood, I just (not to minimize) DIDN'T get it! I missed the money Ball and you suffered. As a mother now, you can Imagine how I must feel for your pain.

Your inner strength and perseverance has allowed you to create, what I hope is a rich, rewarding and fulfilling life. You have a wonderful relationship with ██ and together, you are raising 3 loving children. I admire your parenting and intuitiveness.

Even though I may not have Been as close to you as we Both wanted (and you needed) when you were growing up, I hope over the last several years (especially since you met ██) that our Bond has tightened and that your trust in me as a DAD has Been nurtured. I want you to feel that I love Being with you and your family and sharing your experiences and events.

I can't undo what has been done, or not done, but I can certainly and will be more in tune with your expectations of me. I want you to know that I always think of you with love and joy and am so happy for your nature - exuberance, enthusiasm and joie de vivre. It's contagious and up lifting. Your dynamism is exciting for me, as your dad, to experience and share. How much you have had to overcome to achieve all that you have, so far.

I hope I can live up to my goals of helping you to repair the disappointments you have felt and give you the trusting relationship with your father that you deserve. I certainly am aware of who you are, and how hard you have worked to be close to me and build our relationship.

I can't tell you how pained I am at what you have experienced and how I have disappointed you as you grew up, I want our bond to be strengthened and my sensitivity to your hopes to be on target.

I love you, I adore you,
I want your life to be and
meet all of your expectations

Dad

— 167 —

RESOURCES

Whether you are just beginning the journey to finding your best self or are looking for ways to level up, this section offers a selection of resources designed to help you along the way.

OVERCOMING TRAUMA

The childhood sexual abuse I experienced was devastating, but it did not break me. There is always a way out, no matter what obstacles are in front of you. Here are some books and organizations to check out, whether you're recovering or advocating for someone you love.

National Child Traumatic Stress Network

Offering a benchmark for care, information and resources, this organization caters to traumatized children and their families and communities. *nctsn.org*

National Children's Advocacy Center

The National Children's Advocacy Center offers service, education and leadership around child abuse as well as resources and training for an international audience. *nationalcac.org*

National Sexual Violence Resource Center

Resources for survivors, friends and families, and advocates and educators. *nsvrc.org*

RAINN – Rape, Abuse & Incest National Network

RAINN is the nation's largest anti-sexual violence organization. They operate the National Sexual Assault Hotline – 800-656-4673 – as well as live chat and many programs and resources. *rainn.org*

The Sexual Healing Journey: A Guide for Survivors of Sexual Abuse, by Wendy Maltz

The authoritative guide on recovering from sexual abuse as outlined by this renowned psychotherapist, author and speaker.

Who's the Boss of This Body?, by Meghan Hurley Backofen

Broaching the subject of sexual abuse with children opens up a minefield of potential mishaps. How explicit should you be? What should you cover? This book helps caregivers create a safe space around the issue.

FINDING YOUR BEST SELF

Part inspiration, part kick-in-the-pants, the following are designed to jump-start your journey into glowing up.

Food Matters

Food Matters is committed to helping you help yourself. They believe that your body is worthy of good care and that no one is more suitably qualified to care for it than you are. Think of them as your nutritional consultants and know they are here with you on your journey to a healthier life. *foodmatters.com*

Gaia

Gaia provides exclusive streaming of curated, conscious media content to subscribers through various channels. Topics include transformation, truth seeking, alternative healing and yoga. *gaia.com*

Kripalu Center for Yoga & Health
Kripalu is the largest yoga-based retreat center in North America. Located in the beautiful Berkshires of Massachusetts, Kripalu offers retreats and programs featuring world-class teachers, thinkers, authors and presenters in yoga, meditation, holistic wellness and self-discovery. *kripalu.org*

Louise Hay
Louise Hay is known as one of the founders of the self-help movement. She created a reference guide that details the mental causes of physical ailments and developed positive thought patterns for reversing illness and creating health. The guide became the basis for *Heal Your Body,* also known affectionately as "the little blue book." She travels throughout the US, lecturing and facilitating workshops on loving ourselves and healing our lives. *louisehay.com*

Naturally Yoga
This is my favorite local yoga studio, and the owner, Sheryl Edsall, truly walks the walk. Over the past 20 years, Sheryl has nurtured an amazing community of teachers and healers that looks to support your spiritual evolution regardless of where you are in your process. What I love about Naturally Yoga is that it's a way of life and not a fad meant to replace a gym workout. I consider Naturally Yoga more of a spiritual retreat and a place that offers an old-school yoga studio experience, where you can ground and center yourself and really connect with your inner being. It also offers Reiki, meditation, kirtan, tapping and so much more. If you are looking to explore your spiritual side, this is a haven for beginners as well as people further along in their journey. As a bonus, it offers Zoom options for many of the classes. *naturallyyoga.com*

Tony Robbins

It was Tony Robbins's first book, *Awaken the Giant Within*, that I believe got me started on my healing and self-development journey. *tonyrobbins.com*

Wayne Dyer

Wayne Dyer was an internationally renowned author and speaker in the fields of self-development and spiritual growth. He wrote more than 40 books, including 21 *New York Times* bestsellers, created audio and video programs, and appeared on thousands of television and radio shows. *drwaynedyer.com*

FINDING A THERAPIST

Looking to sort through your past and unpack some of the emotional baggage you've been carrying around? Then it's time to find a good therapist. These sites offer an ideal starting point for finding a therapist you can connect with and who can support you in your healing process.

American Psychological Association (APA)

The APA is the leading scientific and professional organization representing psychology in the United States, with more than 121,000 researchers, educators, clinicians, consultants and students as its members. *apa.org*

Psychology Today

Explore a comprehensive directory of therapists, psychiatrists and treatment facilities near you. *psychologytoday.com*

FINDING A COACH

Looking to move forward in life? Need some motivation to evoke transformation? Want some help to see your own potential? Give coaching a try. Here's where to get started!

Co-Active Training Institute (CTI)
CTI believes everyone is continually moving on a journey of transformation. Founded as the Coaches Training Institute more than 25 years ago, CTI has used the paradigm of coach training to support humanity on that journey. *coactive.com*

International Coaching Federation (ICF)
The ICF offers the only globally recognized, independent credentialing program for coach practitioners and has a listing of coaches who have a proven commitment to integrity, an understanding and mastery of coaching skills, and dedication to clients. *coachingfederation.org*

GIVING BACK
During the course of their lives, my parents made a tremendous impact not just on my life but, thanks to their philanthropic work, on the lives of so many people they would never know. Giving back was crucially important to them, and it is a legacy that lives on in both me and my sister. With that in mind, I invite you to join me in honoring my parents by making a donation to one of their favorite charities, listed here in alphabetical order.

The Doe Fund
The Doe Fund's mission is to break the cycles of homelessness, addiction and criminal recidivism by providing holistic services, housing and work opportunities. *doe.org*

enCourage Kids
The enCourage Kids Foundation envisions a world where every child – regardless of the difficulty of his or her medical journey – experiences joy, hope, resilience and healing. *encourage-kids.org*

Foundation Fighting Blindness
The Foundation Fighting Blindness was established in 1971 with a clear goal: to drive the research that would lead to preventions,

treatments and cures for retinal degenerative diseases – including macular degeneration, retinitis pigmentosa and Usher syndrome. The Foundation is the world's leading private source for inherited retinal disease research funding. *fightingblindness.org*

MORE BOOKS THAT MEAN A LOT TO ME
Breaking the Habit of Being Yourself – Joe Dispenza
The Gifts of Imperfection – Brené Brown
How to Win Friends and Influence People – Dale Carnegie
Intentional Living – John C. Maxwell
Letting Go – David Hawkins
The Power of Now – Eckhart Tolle
The Power of Positive Thinking – Norman Vincent Peale
The Seat of the Soul – Gary Zukav
The Shift – Wayne Dyer
The Untethered Soul – Michael Singer
You Can Heal Your Life – Louise Hay